YEAR OF THE DUCK

a play by
ISRAEL HOROVITZ

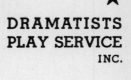

DRAMATISTS
PLAY SERVICE
INC.

Dramatists Play Service

ESTABLISHED BY MEMBERS OF THE

DRAMATISTS' GUILD OF THE AUTHORS' LEAGUE OF AMERICA

for the

HANDLING OF THE ACTING RIGHTS

OF MEMBERS' PLAYS

and

THE ENCOURAGEMENT OF THE AMERICAN THEATRE

THE LAST WORD IN MAKE-UP

A Practical Illustrated Handbook

By DR. RUDOLPH LISZT

Revised Edition

A work for all who use make-up on the stage, in the class-room, in the photographer's studio, and TV stations. Compact and easy to understand, it is pre-eminently practical. It is one of the most completely illustrated works issued on this art, containing 44 half-tone photographs (unretouched) and over 80 original drawings by the author, who has been make-up artist for major motion picture studios.

Press Comments

"THE LAST WORD IN MAKE-UP *is the only book on the subject containing a complete, easily followed chart that offers at a glance instructions for the creation of hundreds of parts and characters from A to Z.*"

— FILM DAILY

"[*Dr. Liszt's*] *book* THE LAST WORD IN MAKE-UP . . . *is required reading in most drama departments. . . .*"

— ORLANDO SENTINEL

One paper volume $6.00

440 PARK AVENUE SOUTH   **NEW YORK, N. Y. 10016**

YEAR OF THE DUCK

a play by
ISRAEL HOROVITZ

**DRAMATISTS
PLAY SERVICE
INC.**

SOUND EFFECTS RECORDS

The following sound effects records, which may be used in connection with production of this play, can be obtained from Thomas J. Valentino, Inc., 151 West 46th Street, New York, N.Y. 10036.

No. 5025 — Door bell
No. 5041 — Auto sounds
No. 5177 — Gunshots

SPECIAL NOTE ON SONGS AND MUSIC

For performance of such songs and music mentioned in this play as are in copyright, the permission of the copyright owners must be obtained; or other songs and music in the public domain substituted.

For Gill.

ISRAEL HOROVITZ (*Author*) was born in Wakefield, Massachusetts, in 1939. His first play, *The Comeback*, was written at age 17. In the years since, more than thirty Horovitz plays have been translated and produced in more than twenty languages, worldwide. Among his best-known plays are: *The Indian Wants the Bronx; Line* (which just celebrated its thirteenth anniversary of continuous performance, off Broadway); *It's Called the Sugar Plum; Rats; Morning* (of Broadway's *Morning, Noon and Night*); *The Wakefield Plays*, a seven-play cycle including *Hopscotch, The 75th Alfrea the Great, Our Father's Failing, Alfred Dies, Stage Directions,* and *Spared; Mackerel; The Primary Class;* and *The Good Parts.* Other Horovitz plays that have been seen In NYC during the past few seasons include the trilogy: *Today; I am a Fountain Pen; A Rosen by Any Other Name;* and *The Chopin Playoffs.* For the past several years, Horovitz has been at work on a cycle of Gloucester, Massachusetts-based plays, all of which have had their world premiers at the Gloucester Stage Company, founded by Horovitz nine years ago. Among Horovitz's Gloucester plays are: *The Widow's Blind Date; Park Your Car in Harvard Square; North Shore Fish,* which had its NYC premiere last season at the WPA Theater, where it won nominations for both the Pulitzer Prize and the Drama Desk Award; *Firebird at Dogtown; Sunday Runners in the Rain,* which had its NYC premiere at the Public Theater; and *Year of the Duck,* which premiered as a collaboration of the Gloucester Stage Company, the Portland (Maine) Stage Company, and the Hudson Guild Theatre. For film, Horovitz has written *The Strawberry Statement; Author! Author!;* and *A Man in Love.* For television, Horovitz adapted "Bartleby, the Scrivener;" "A Day with Conrad Green;" and wrote and directed "Play for Germs" for VD Blues. He has won numerous awards, including two Obies, the Emmy, the French Critic's Prize, the Los Angeles Critics' Prize, the New York Drama Desk Award, the Vernon Rice Award, the Christopher Award, an Award in Literature of the American Academy of Arts and Letters, the Prix du Jury of the Cannes Film Festival, the Prix Italia, and the Eliot Norton Award for his contribution to theatre in Boston. Horovitz is founder and artistic director of the New York Playwrights Lab, and serves the Gloucester Stage Company as its artistic director. He is married to marathoner Gillian Adams-Horovitz. He is the father of five children. The Horovitz family divides its time among homes in Gloucester, Massachusetts; New York City; and Dulwich, England.

(April, 1988)

ABOUT *THE WILD DUCK*

The story of Henrik Ibsen's *The Wild Duck* centers around the
Ekdahl family: Hjalmar; his wife, Gina; and his fourteen-year-old
daughter, Hedvig. Hjalmar's father also lives with them in their
apartment, which is connected to his photographic studio. In the
back of the studio they have fashioned a sort of wildlife menagerie
which includes rabbits, various birds, and a wild duck.

Hjalmar's old friend, Gregers Werle, has just returned to town,
after a fifteen-year absence. On returning, he finds that Hjalmar and
Gina are married, the match having been arranged by Haakon
Werle, Gregers' father. Gregers, knowing his father and Gina had
an affair fifteen years earlier, sets about the task of enlightening his
friend Hjalmar to the truth, believing the truth will set him free to
build a new life together with Gina, based on the ideal.

Gregers' interference, however, backfires when Hjalmar does
not strive for the truth of the ideal, and rejects Gina and his home.
Matters are made more complicated by the fact that Hedvig is going
blind due to a hereditary illness. Haaken Werle is also going blind.
Hjalmar puts the pieces together and confronts Gina, asking her if
Hedvig is his child. She answers that she does not know, and
Hjalmar in turn rejects Hedvig.

In a conversation with Hedvig, Gregers tells her the way to win
back Hjalmar's love is to sacrifice that which she loves most, the wild
duck, in order to prove the truth of her love for her father.

Hedvig takes her grandfather's gun into the back to shoot the
wild duck. There is a gunshot. Instead of shooting the duck, Hedvig
has killed herself.

YEAR OF THE DUCK was first presented as a collaborative production of three theatres: the Portland Stage Company (Barbara Rosoff, Artistic Director), the Gloucester Stage Company (Israel Horovitz, Artistic Director), and the Hudson Guild Theatre (Geoffrey Sherman, Producing Director).

The Portland Stage Company production opened on March 11, 1987 in Portland, Maine. It was directed by Barbara Rosoff; the scenery was by Patricia Woodbridge; the costumes were by Mimi Maxmen; the lighting was by Jackie Manassee; the production stage manager was Rheatha Forster; the assistant stage manager was J. Elizabeth Sand; and the casting was by Elissa Myers and Mark Teschner. The cast, in order of appearance, was as follows:

SOPHIE BUDD . . . . Heather Willihnganz
HARRY BUDD . . . . James Huston
MARGARET BUDD . . . . Ann-Sara Matthews
NATHAN BUDD . . . . Bernie Pesseltiner
JOHN SHARP . . . . Roscoe Born
ROSIE NORRIS . . . . Lisa Emery

The Gloucester Stage Company production opened on July 17, 1988 in Gloucester, Massachusetts. It was directed by Geoffrey Sherman; the costume design was by Mimi Maxmen; the scenic/light design was by Patrick J. Scully; and the production stage manager was Fredrick Hahn. The cast, in order of appearance, was as follows:

SOPHIE . . . . Heather Willihnganz
HARRY . . . . James Huston
MARGARET . . . . Ann-Sara Matthews
NATHAN . . . . Bernie Pesseltiner
JOHN . . . . Paul O'Brien
ROSIE . . . . Jan Connery

The Hudson Guild Theatre production opened October 7, 1988 in New York City. It was directed by Geoffrey Sherman; the set and light design was by Paul Wonsek; the costume design was by Mimi Maxmen; and the stage manager was Fredrick Hahn. The cast, in order of appearance, was as follows:

THE PEOPLE OF THE PLAY

SOPHIE BUDD, 14, extremely cute, extremely bright; a natural performer; an innocent; kitten.

HARRY BUDD, 30's; baby-faced, cute; somewhat helpless; a natural performer; an innocent; lazy peacock.

MARGARET BUDD, 30's; thin, mysterious; ironic, reticent, self-sufficient; hen-hawk.

ROSIE NORRIS, 30's; ex-cheerleader looks; once a bombshell, now top of age category, locally; stutters when not being theatrical; show-pony.

NATHAN BUDD, indeterminately old; Yankee-Jew, baby-faced, somewhat helpless; a natural performer; as innocent; old goat (formerly cutest goat in litter).

JOHN SHARP, 30's; large, but without great physical strength; mysterious, dark; buzzard.

THE PLACE OF THE PLAY

Budd family's home, Gloucester, Massachusetts.

THE TIME OF THE PLAY

The present, approximately one hundred years after the world premiere of Henrik Ibsen's *The Wild Duck*.

THE ACCENT OF THE PLAY

North Shore Massachusetts ("Pah'k Yo'r Ca'h Wick'id Ahwful") accent required for all characters at all times.

THE MUSIC OF THE PLAY

Show tunes, before and after each scene. Important that "Comedy Tonight" be used before final scene of play. Possibilities for other scenes: "There's No Business Like Show Business;" "Another Opening, Another Show;" "Some People;" "Broken Hearts on Broadway;" etc.*

*See Special Note on copyright page.

THE ACCENT OF THE PLAY

THE MUSIC OF THE PLAY

YEAR OF THE DUCK

ACT I
Scene 1

Gloucester, Massachusetts, the present, evening.

Darkness in auditorium. No sound.

Suddenly, the giggling of a girl, Sophie, joined by the laughter of a man, her father, Harry Budd.

SOPHIE. Hurry!
HARRY. Hold still!
SOPHIE. Hurry! Hurry!
HARRY. Two shakes! This thing hasn't been used in years!
SOPHIE. Hurry! Hurry!
HARRY. Hold it! Hold it!

(Suddenly, an explosion of light. A photograph has been taken in an old-fashioned way: an explosion of phosphorous; puff of smoke; and stage lights joining in, on switch. The play has begun. Sophie stands, facing old-fashioned camera. She wears an old-fashioned dress. She hugs a duck in her arms. She wears empty eyeglass frames. Harry laughs, waves at the smoke cloud in the room. He wears blue jeans and a Wingaersheek Players T-shirt. Harry and Sophie are extremely affectionate with one another, easily so. They are an enviably attractive father/daughter set. The Budd family home is on two levels. The first level is fairly standard; dining room, door to sun room, kitchen, back door, hall to front door, all in evidence. Centerpiece round oak table, set C. under over-sized, old-fashioned Tiffany globe, brilliantly colored. The upstairs setting is far more unique, as the upper attic has been opened to the eaves and

11

the result is a severly A-framed space, punctuated with huge skylights over the main space. R. is Budd's darkroom. L. is door to Sophie's bedroom and door to Nathan's bedroom. The Budd family's photographic studio is replete with both modern and antique equipment. Dozens of photos are tacked to walls in chaotic fashion, most are photos of plays. Huge rolls of beautifully colored "no-seam" background papers are in evidence, hanging down from racks mounted on the rear wall. By pulling down this roll or that, Budd is able to alter the background to any setup easily. At the play's opening, a bright pink paper is pulled down, in joyous contrast to Sophie's pale yellow dress. The expanse of pink creates backdrop for this opening scene.)

SOPHIE. Oh, God, I'm blind! The smell is gross... *(Hugs the duck to calm him.)* Don't be scared, don't be scared... *(To Harry.)* You got the duck terrified...

HARRY. The duck's fine... *(Harry kisses the duck.)* Tell her you're fine... *("Talks" as the duck, as might a ventriloquist.)* I'm fine, Sophie. I'm a tough duck!

SOPHIE. *(Hugs duck all the more. False concern.)* Ohhh, Daddy, don't kid. He's shaking wicked... *(To duck.)* Don't shake, Oliver...

HARRY. You can't call a duck "Oliver."

SOPHIE. Why not?

HARRY. It's no name for a duck.

SOPHIE. How about "Ollie"? Ollie's cute...

HARRY. It's *too* cute. It's like a TV duck. This is no TV duck. The is a *real* duck... *(Takes duck's foot in his hand; shakes it like a hand; false macho voice.)* This is a *man's* duck. *("Throws duck voice.)* You bet your ass I'm a man's duck! *(Scolding voice, confidential; to duck.)* Watch your mouth! There's a kid! *("Throws" duck's voice, again.)* Sorry, sorry...I'm kind of a *dirty* duck... *(Sophie giggles. Margaret enters from kitchen, carrying plates of food. The table is set for three places. She sets food down, quickly, burning her fingers; does a little dance, shaking off the pain. Margaret is Harry's age; equally attractive. They were Gloucester High School's cutest couple, fifteen years prior. She calls upstairs.)*

12

MARGARET. You almost ready?

HARRY. I see this duck as "Max."

SOPHIE. I hate Max.

HARRY. What's the matter with Max?

SOPHIE. He picks his nose in English.

MARGARET. Are you two almost ready?

HARRY. *(Calls down to Margaret.)* We haven't printed it yet! *(To Sophie.)* Is "He picks his nose in English" a manner of speaking, as in "I prefer my opera in Italian"?

SOPHIE. No, it's a matter of fact, as in "Max Linsky picks his nose in English..."

MARGARET. Everything's ready!

HARRY. Five minutes, Margaret!

MARGARET. But, everything's ready!

HARRY. I can do it in three minutes! You don't wanna' let these old plates sit around!

MARGARET. Come downstairs, Sophie!

SOPHIE. I wanna watch!

MARGARET. Come downstairs! He'll never finish with you with him!

HARRY. Go down with your mother...

SOPHIE. Nooo, Poppy. I wanna' watch!

MARGARET. Sophie!

SOPHIE. *(To Harry.)* I wanna' watch, Poppy...

HARRY. Let her watch, Peg, huh? I only hav'ta get an image. Two minutes, really! It's for the poster!

MARGARET. Just hurry it up...

SOPHIE. Thanks, Mama... *(Flashes conspiratorial look at Harry, who smiles at his daughter; calls to wife.)*

HARRY. Two minutes... *(Harry and Sophie move into darkroom. Red bulb lights on exterior of darkroom, onstage, indicating darkroom is is use. Downstairs, Nathan Budd enters from TV Room; goes to Margaret.*

NATHAN. What's the yelling?

MARGARET. There's no yelling.

NATHAN. I didn't wake up from no-yelling. I woke up from yelling.

13

MARGARET. *(To Nathan, as she exits into kitchen.)* You shouldn't sleep at six, anyhow. You'll be waking up in the middle of the night, again.

NATHAN. *(He samples food.)* I wasn't sleeping. I was dozing... *(Margaret returns from kitchen carrying two other plates of food. She sets plates down on table, burning fingers. She scolds Nathan without looking at him.)*

MARGARET. Don't sample!

NATHAN. I'm not sampling. I'm eating. *(Margaret exits again into kitchen. Nathan calls after her.)* Who's not eating?

MARGARET. *(Offstage.)* I ate, already.

NATHAN. When?

MARGARET. *(Offstage.)* Before.

NATHAN. While you were cooking?

MARGARET. *(Enters.)* What's the difference?

NATHAN. I'm just interested. When you were cooking, or in between?

MARGARET. I'm not allowed any more food.

NATHAN. Says Pritikin?

MARGARET. Says Pritikin.

NATHAN. The man committed suicide.

MARGARET. He was thin.

NATHAN. Now he's thinner.

MARGARET. Sit down, Nathan. Eat it while it's hot.

NATHAN. You're not going to be agoraphobic, are you?

MARGARET. You mean "anorexic." Agoraphobic means "a dread of going to the market place." Anorexic means "starving yourself"...

NATHAN. It's hard to keep the diseases straight, anymore. They have a movie about a different disease on TV every night, some-times two a night. I think they invent diseases... *(Samples; smiles.)* Your mother-in-law invented a disease: "Agoraphobo-Reverso." She suffered from it all her life...

MARGARET. What's Agoraphobo-Reverso?

NATHAN. A dread of *leaving* the market place.

MARGARET. The thing of it is, I actually paid rapt attention.

14

NATHAN. Why not? You think I don't rapt my attention on you? Where are they? *(Goes to staircase, screams.)* Harold and Sophie! Your supper's on the table!

MARGARET. Don't, Nathan...

NATHAN. Harold!

MARGARET. Pa! I asked you not to... *(Nathan turns, looks at Margaret.)*

NATHAN. It's a hot cooked meal...It'll go cold.

MARGARET. It's my business.

NATHAN. It's my business, too, thank you. I'd like to get some sleep in the late afternoons...

MARGARET. It'll turn out.

NATHAN. Of course it'll turn out. You're a smart girl, Margaret...That's why we married you. *(Smiles. There is a pause between them. Margaret looks up at Nathan, smiles; then Nathan continues, softly.)* In forty-one years of marriage (May God Treat Her Kindly in Heaven nevertheless) she hot-cooked possibly four meals...

MARGARET. Pa! C'mon...

NATHAN. She had other strong points...

MARGARET. She worked.

NATHAN. She did not work! She taught! I think we should keep the distinction clear. She did not work. She taught. *(Samples.)* These noodles are nice. *(Margaret turns away, lost in thought. Nathan sees her; watches a moment. Margaret looks out window. Margaret senses his staring; turns, smiles.)*

MARGARET. Those aren't noodles, Pa. It's Fettucine Alfredo.

NATHAN. Don't ask me. *(Shrugs.)* How would *I* know? *(Motions to window.)* Somebody out there? *(Looks.)* Pitch-black...

MARGARET. Just the wind.

NATHAN. Gets dark too early. You never see sunlight...3:30, 4 o'clock...

MARGARET. Winter.

NATHAN. What's their play about that they're shooting the poster for?

MARGARET. *The Wild Duck?* I haven't read it yet.

NATHAN. You'd better, else you won't know what to expect. Whenever she was acting in a play, life would take some enormous turn, usually *bad!* I never knew what the hell was goin' on...until I read the play. *(Samples food.)* Plays are dangerous. I remember, growing up, my mother used'ta say "Literature never hurt anybody!" Then when I was about nine, I heard about some lunatic who read *Gone with the Wind* and burned his house down. What about that? *(Samples; nods smugly.)* My mother was crazy! There is nothing on the face of the earth that's more dangerous than literature. Take it from me. *(Suddenly.)* I'm starving here! This is ridiculous! I'm calling him down!

MARGARET. No! Stay out of it!

NATHAN. *Harold!*

MARGARET. Nathan, damn it!

NATHAN. *I'm starving, here... You think you live alone? (Margaret is upset. She goes to sink. Nathan senses her upset; calls across to her.)* What do *I* know? I'm an old man... *(The lights widen to include upstairs, again. We hear Sophie's giggles. The door opens to the darkroom and Sophie exits, laughing. She calls downstairs.)*

SOPHIE. It's great, Mummy! It's a great picture! It's gonna be a wicked brilliant poster! Poppy is a genius photographer. *(Sophie runs down the stairs to Margaret and Nathan. Harry exits the darkroom, reaches behind; switching out red light, shutting.)* The duck is smiling. You can see. He's so *cute! (To Nathan.)* How do you like "Sheldon"?

NATHAN. I had a cousin Sheldon.

SOPHIE. That shouldn't matter...

NATHAN. I think he's still alive.

SOPHIE. It's a sweet name for a duck...

NATHAN. You can't use Sheldon. It's against Jewish Law to name somebody after somebody who's still alive.

SOPHIE. Even a duck?

NATHAN. *Especially* a duck. Pick another name.

SOPHIE. I'm only a quarter Jewish.

NATHAN. The other three quarters don't count. Pick another name.

16

SOPHIE. Poppy wants Max.

NATHAN. I also had a cousin Max, but he's dead, so Max is available.

SOPHIE. I *loathe* Max.

MARGARET. What's the matter with Max?

SOPHIE. Don't ask. It's too gross around food. Can I start?

MARGARET. Sure.

SOPHIE. *(Calls out.)* Poppy! *(Harry exits an upstairs bathroon, wiping his hands on his trousers; carelessly. He bounds down the staircase; suddenly winces.)*

HARRY. Oh, shit!

MARGARET. Your knee?   SOPHIE. You okay, Poppy?

HARRY. Shit, shit, shit!

MARGARET. Is it out?   NATHAN. Watch your mouth, will you?

HARRY. Nearly. *(Hobbles to table; sits. To Margaret.)* You're not eating?

MARGARET. I ate already.

HARRY. She stopped eating.

MARGARET. I didn't stop eating.

HARRY. I never see you eat...

MARGARET. That's 'cause you're never home. I do all my eating home. Come home once in a while. I'll *munch* for you...

HARRY. I slept down at the shop two nights...big deal.

SOPHIE. You should eat, Mama. It's really delicious...

MARGARET. I've already *eaten!*

NATHAN. *(Lightening the load.)* You know what Mahatma Gandhi's wife said to him after the nineteenth day of his hunger strike?

HARRY. This'll be rich.

NATHAN. "Come onnn, Mahatmaaah, eatt soemthinggg, a cookie, even! Who's gonna know?"

SOPHIE. Oh, *Gandhi* was a great, great movie!

HARRY. *(To Margaret.)* Will you pass me some noodles, or what? Just 'cause you quit eating, doesn't mean everybody has to! *(Margaret shoves the casserole across the table at Harry, gruffly; wordlessly. Harry says the following with an embarrassed smile.)* She

17

serves my supper like a subpoena! *(There is a small, worried silence. Margaret is very, very unhappy. She turns D., away from Harry and Sophie, to hide her hurt. Nathan sees her and is concerned. Sophie senses what's going on and tries to save the moment; breaks the silence; brightly.)*

SOPHIE. Miss Hogan made me tell the whole class about the play. I nearly *died*...I had to stand up and make this whole speech. I was *sooo wick'id embarrassed!* Miss Hogan's so old everybody says her brain's gone... *(Suddenly.)* Sorry, Grandpa.

NATHAN. I've known Kathleen Hogan since she started teachin'...Her brain was gone, then, too...

SOPHIE. Miss Hogan says if I have one eighth of Grandma Budd's talent, I could be a great actress...

NATHAN. *(Smiles.)* If you wanna' be a *great* actress, you have to eat your Alfredo Fettucine...

SOPHIE. It's fabulous Fettucine! Was Grandma Lynch a great cook, too, Mama?

MARGARET. Grandma Lynch was more of an *enthusiastic* cook than a great cook...

HARRY. Pass the noodles. We ought to get your mother to cook duck de l'orange.

SOPHIE. Poppppyyy!! That's not funnyyy!

HARRY. Seems fair enough to me: we feed the duck for awhile then he feeds us...

SOPHIE. Poppppyyy!

HARRY. At least we'd know we were doing a tragedy...if the title-role character ends up dead...

SOPHIE. It's hard to tell if we're acting in a comedy or a tragedy...

NATHAN. Do the funny parts. If the audience doesn't laugh, you've got a tragedy on your hands...

HARRY. It's a serious problem. The play got terrible, terrible reviews when it first came out...'cause nobody could tell whether it was a tragedy or a comedy.

NATHAN. To me, the difference between comedy and tragedy depends on who falls down the stairs. If the other guy falls down the stairs, that's a *comedy*. If I fall down the stairs, that'a definite *tragedy*.

MARGARET. What happens if everybody falls down the stairs?

NATHAN. *A lawyer's dream!*

HARRY. It's all in how the thing ends. That's what I think. If it's got a happy ending: that's a comedy. If it's got an unhappy ending...

MARGARET. *(Interjects ironically.)* Brilliant.

HARRY. ...that's a tragedy. *(Flashes look at wristwatch.)* They're late already.

NATHAN. They're coming here.

SOPHIE. We have to rehearse, Grandpa! We've only been rehearsing sixteen weeks! Old Mr. Sims is sick all the time, too. He misses so many rehearsals...

NATHAN. He's comin' here?

SOPHIE. He's *sick!* I just *said* that. You should have played the part, Grandpa. You would have been really *great!*

NATHAN. I gave up acting. I promised your grandmother on her deathbed that I'd never act again. Look, I think it's great you're doin' the play together — the whole buncha ya's — I just don't like the idea of ya's rehearsin' here, in the house. You don't do plays where you live.

SOPHIE. But, *why?*

MARGARET. He's got his TV show. What's on tonight, Pa? Third episode?

NATHAN. Fourth. It all ends in two weeks. And I hate it when you change the subject on me that way!

MARGARET. Are they all coming?

HARRY. Why?

MARGARET. Just wondering...

HARRY. Rosie and John...

MARGARET. That's all?

HARRY. A subtext session: Just key principals...and the director.

NATHAN. Who's directing?

19

HARRY. John Sharp. John's directing and playing Gregers, the mean one...he loves the play, so, he does both: directs and acts. And he did the scenery, too, a'course...

SOPHIE. I've got to change into my costume. Leave my plate, Mama, and I'll wash it later... *(Sophie exits up stairs. Harry stands; starts off.)*

HARRY. I should look at my lines, too. Leave my plate and I'll do it, after...

MARGARET. Sure... *(Harry exits up stairs. There is a moment's pause.)*

NATHAN. I'll help you clear...

MARGARET. I don't mind. You'd better get to your show...

NATHAN. There's time... *(He stands; starts to clear table.)*

MARGARET. Leave it, Nathan, really... *(Pause.)* It'll give me something to do... *(There is another small pause.)*

NATHAN. You should watch with me. I could fill you in on what you've missed.

MARGARET. It's okay. I'm kind of tired.

NATHAN. Oh! Did anybody remember to feed the duck?

MARGARET. Sophie did, right after school...

NATHAN. We should have a better system...Yesterday, we both fed him...

MARGARET. If he wasn't hungry, he wouldn't have eaten...

NATHAN. You don't *know* that...Maybe they eat whatever's put in front of them. Some animals...me, for example. I eat whatever crap you put in front of me... (It was excellent, first-rate Alfredo, really. I loved it. That's not what I meant...) Who knows about ducks, really? Maybe ducks gorge...

MARGARET. *(Smiles; the doorbell rings.)* They're here...

SOPHIE. *(Yells from upstairs.)* They're here! *(Harry bounds down the stairs; through the room and off, to the door.)*

HARRY. *(As he passes through the room.)* They're here...

NATHAN. *(After a pause; with a shrug; smiling.)* They're here.

HARRY. *(Offstage.)* Hey, both of you! You come together?

ROSIE. *(Offstage.)* John picked me up...

JOHN. *(Offstage.)* Saves a car... *Sophie bounds down the stairs. She's*

20

changed her clothing and is now slightly dressed up. She's excited.)

SOPHIE. They come in yet?

NATHAN. Just.

SOPHIE. *(Goes to Margaret.)* I wish you would work on the show — be on, you know, the *inside...*

MARGARET. It's not for me...I'm no good at acting. I tried it...

SOPHIE. You wouldn't have to *act.* You could stage-manage ...do props...

MARGARET. It's not for me...

SOPHIE. I wish you were part of it...Hi Mr. Sharp!

JOHN. *(Enters.)* Hi, Soph...Hi, Peg. Hullo, Mr. Budd...

ROSIE. *(Offstage.)* Just takin' my boots off!

MARGARET. Hello, John...How's Allison?

JOHN. Flu.

MARGARET. That's bad luck...

JOHN. Bad winter...

MARGARET. How're the twins?

JOHN. Great, really. 'Course, you know, twins kinda' pass those germs back and forth...back and forth...back and forth... *(He smiles at his small joke.)*

MARGARET. Well, it's really great to see you again. It's be'n a long time...

JOHN. A *long* time.

MARGARET. I was just thinkin' that...

JOHN. Five years...

MARGARET. Noooo!

JOHN. Yup.

MARGARET. Gawwd! *(There is a pause as they stare at one another. Nathan breaks into the silence.)*

NATHAN. How's your father?

JOHN. My father's, uh, well...he passed away...

NATHAN. *(Alarmed.)* My god! When?

JOHN. Twenty years ago. I think you're confusing me with my cousins, Austin and the other John Sharp... *(Smiles.)* There are two John Sharps. The other one lives down Prospect Street...

NATHAN. *(Confused.)* 'Course... *(Pauses.)* Your mother's still, uh...?

JOHN. Oh, *totally!* I just saw her before I picked Rosie up. She lives over my ma's why, so, I figured "Why not take a whack at two birds?" Visit my ma and pick up my star.*

NATHAN. "One stone" kinda' thing, you mean?

JOHN. Exactly!

ROSIE. Hiiii! *(Enters. Rosie wears layers of dark clothing. Her skirt is long, as is her coat-sweater, which she removes as she enters. She also wears a full shawl and baggy peasant-like overblouse. The effect is quite theatrical. She sees Sophie. She unpacks a Wingaersheek Players sweatshirt which she gives to Sophie.)* Hiiii Sophie!!!

SOPHIE. *(Runs to Rosie; hugs her. They kiss both cheeks, saying "Moi, moi!" — in "actressy" fashion.)* Hiii, Rosie! *(Lines from The Wild Duck, in Norwegian.)* Det var rigtig godt, at bedstefar fik alt det al skrive igen.

ROSIE. *(Answers in Norwegian, from the same play.)* Jaaa, stakkers famle far; sa tjener han sig da en liden lommeskilling...

JOHN. *(Proudly.)* Perfect! *(Sophie hugs Rosie affectionately.)*

NATHAN. What's this?

MARGARET. Their play.

ROSIE. *(Slightly embarrassed by the girls affection, searches for then finds Margaret; hugs her.)* Hi, MMMMM...Margie**

MARGARET. Hi, Rosie. How's Earl?

ROSIE. Fat. Mean. Same as ever...

MARGARET. How's Little Earl?

ROSIE. Dead. Everybody looks around at Rosie's grotesque joke. Rosie whoops with laughter.) Just checking to see if you were all paying attention.

JOHN. *(Laughs.)* She does that to me all the time! Last week she said her mother drowned...

NATHAN. What's this?

ROSIE. Just my weird sense of humor...How are you, Mr. Budd?

---

*NOTE: "Ma" and "star" rhyme, perfectly, with use of Massachusetts accent.
**NOTE: Hard "G" - Marg*h*ee.

NATHAN. Fine, fine, Rosie. Still snowing out?

ROSIE. Wicked. Earl's been plowing all day. Extra money with the truck kind of thing...

NATHAN. *(To Margaret.)* Who's Earl?

MARGARET. Earl Norris, Rosie's husband...

NATHAN. Nig Norris' boy?

ROSIE. Cousin. Earl's father's Dusty...

NATHAN. In what sense?

ROSIE. That's his name! Dusty!

NATHAN. Oh, God, Dusty Norris! From Eastern Avenue School District...

ROSIE. Kind of. Dusty lives more central. Nearer the old Junior High.

NATHAN. Some Norris lived right up back'a Eastern Avenue School. I used'ta deliver their pap'uh...

JOHN. That was Porker *Morris*...

NATHAN. Who's Porker Morris?

JOHN. Lived back'a Eastern Avenue School...

HARRY. *(Enters.)* Who's this?

JOHN. Where did Porker Morris live?

HARRY. Growin' up? Back'a Eastern Ave Schoolyard...

JOHN. There...What was his father's name?

HARRY. Same as Porker. Porker was a Junior...same as you.

NATHAN. I never knew any Porker...

HARRY. Richard!

JOHN. Richard!

ROSIE. Richard Parker Morris, Junior...

JOHN. Dickie!

JOHN and ROSIE. Dickie-Parker-Pecker-Porker! *(Harry runs and covers Sophie's eyes, as John and Rosie act out vaguely obscene junior high school pantomime of Dickie-Parker-Pecker-Porker's name. All share laugh they've shared before. Nathan is momentarily befuddled.)*

NATHAN. *(Comes the dawn.) Dickie* Morris! With the funny hats! You're married to Dickie Morris's son?

HARRY. She is.

23

ROSIE. I'm not! He's kidding you. I'm married to Dusty *Norris'* son, Earl. From Dale Street...

NATHAN. The fireman?

ROSIE. The fireman's son. Earl's father's father. My husband, Earl Norris, his father was Dusty, who worked down Pat's VW pullin' dents...*his* father was Pally Norris, the fireman. *(And here the "musical" section concludes.)*

NATHAN. *(Lying.)* Of course! *(Smiles to Rosie.)* Well, good to see you all again. If you'll excuse me, I've got a show to watch...Six episodes...Tonight's number four...

JOHN. Robert Frost?

NATHAN. How so?

JOHN. The show you're watchin'...

NATHAN. Oscar Wilde.

JOHN. Oh, right... *(To all.)* I knew it was on a western writer...

SOPHIE. Isn't Robert Frost from around here, somewhere?

MARGARET. Springfield.

JOHN. *(To Margaret, proudly.)* I've just re-read our indigenous poets... *(There are exchanged glances and smiles, all around. John continues.)* Allison's watching, religiously. She's hooked. She says it's good...*different.* Exposes the great homosexual dilemma.

HARRY. Is *that* what the show's about?

NATHAN. To tell you the truth, I haven't been paying close attention...The acting's good.

SOPHIE. I have school tomorrow...

HARRY. We should start...

JOHN. Right.

NATHAN. I'll be seein' you all later. *(He exits into sun room, closing door.)*

JOHN. *(First to Nathan; then to Harry.)* Enjoy...uh, what's his name?

HARRY. My father?

JOHN. *(Calls into sun room.)* The poet...Wilde! Enjoy Oscar Wilde, Mr. Budd!

ROSIE. It's nice of you to put up with us, Peg...

MARGARET. Oh, I don't mind...

JOHN. You should work on the show with us.

MARGARET. Oh, well, I don't think so...

HARRY. Shall we go up? We're gonna actually work in the studio...

ROSIE. That'll be really great!

SOPHIE. I'm going upstairs to fix my hair! *(She runs upstairs into her bedroom.)*

ROSIE. *(Pauses on the stairs.)* You comin' up, Peg? Watch some rehearsal?

MARGARET. Me? No, I'm kinda tired.

HARRY. You can leave the dishes.

MARGARET. Don't worry. *(Harry and Rosie run upstairs; then call down.)*

HARRY. *(To Rosie, quite loudly.)* ...I'll show you around upstairs. You've never been to our house, have you?

ROSIE. Not since I was a very little girl... *(Harry leads Rosie upstairs; they kiss and run into darkroom giggling. John pauses a moment. Looks at Margaret. They have a small shared private moment.)*

JOHN. *(He struggles to find great advective.)* You look... *lovely*...really lovely.

MARGARET. Yuh, thanks.

JOHN. You do. *(Confidentially.)* I wish you'd've auditioned for this, really. You would'a been *fabulous!* *(Margaret goes into kitchen with dinner plates. John follows.)*

MARGARET. How does it feel?

JOHN. Hmm?

MARGARET. Being back.

JOHN. In what sense?

MARGARET. In town? Back home...

JOHN. Back home in town? In Gloucester?

MARGARET. Gloucester...home...in your house, with Allison and the girls...

JOHN. *(Proudly; theatrically.)* Oh, well. I made my choice.

MARGARET. And I was glad, too. I saw Allison...several

25

times...while you were gone and all...

JOHN. Why?

MARGARET. Why did I see her? *(John nods.)* She'd walk by the shop, or I'd bump into her down to C.V.S., or somesuch. It's a small town... *(Pauses.)* She missed you.

JOHN. She told you that?

MARGARET. I could tell. Women can tell things about other women. She missed you a lot. Kids at home, no father, it's not, well, you know...*natural*...

JOHN. *(Looks at Margaret for a moment; he kisses her.)* Are you happy?

MARGARET. *(Stopped; she will babble.)* I'm alright. The shop still does well enough. We do the graduation pictures, still, for the high school. We do Rockport and Ipswich, too... *(Fussing about.)* It's a lot of work, especially from March, on...Eight hundred to a thousand portraits, all in eight weeks' time...all hand-tinted. Still and all. It pays the rent. And the building pays, too... *(She busily scrapes food from dinner plates into garbage bin - foot pedal variety - set up at kitchen table.)*

JOHN. Downtown?

MARGARET. Sure. My father-in-law paid very little for it and rents have, you know...

JOHN. Skyrocketed.

MARGARET. Exactly. *(Smiles.)* We split it up into six apartments, plus our shop and the launderette...

JOHN. You and Harry opened a launderette, too?

MARGARET. Us? Oh, no. We just rent out the space where the Christian Science Reading Room used'ta be...

JOHN. So...they closed up the Christian Science Reading Room?

MARGARET. Business is off all over town...

JOHN. That's what everyone's sayin', yuh. Cigarette? *(John lights two cigarettes and offers her one.)*

MARGARET. I quit.

JOHN. I'm trying to quit myself. *(John throws pack into garbage can under sink.)*

26

MARGARET. *(Fussing about; not looking at John at all.)* You enjoy bein' away?

JOHN. *(Suddenly, he takes charge.)* Sit down and shut up!

MARGARET. Why?

JOHN. Please? *(She does.)* I was alone a lot.

MARGARET. And you liked that?

JOHN. I did, very much, yuh.

MARGARET. Allison and the girls must be glad you're back.

JOHN. They seem to be.

MARGARET. And you?

JOHN. It's different. I was in the woods a lot...walkin'...fishin', sometimes...thinking, constantly. It was an *ascetic* time, the five years...thinking, communing with nature kind of thing. Ascetically.

MARGARET. But, not natural...

JOHN. In what sense?

MARGARET. Family. *(Smiles.)* They must be a lot happier.

JOHN. Are you?

MARGARET. Happier?

JOHN. Mm.

MARGARET. Than when?

JOHN. Than when I wasn't here...home...around. *(There is a pause between them.)*

MARGARET. You better go up.

JOHN. I want to tell you something, Margaret...

MARGARET. You'd better go up... *(Flashes look to TV room door.)* Please. *(Sophie finishes setting up upstairs.)*

SOPHIE. Where are you guys. *(Harry and Rosie's heads pop out of the darkroom.)*

HARRY. We're in here.

SOPHIE. Why?

HARRY. Uh, I showed Rosie the poster.

ROSIE. It's marvelous. *(Downstairs. John and Margaret exchange a knowing glance, as they stop and listen to the intentionally loud chatter above. Margaret looks at John, smiles; shrugs.)*

JOHN. Are you sad about something? *(John moves closer to Margaret.)*

MARGARET. *(Pulling away from him.)* Jesus, Jack! *Don't!*

JOHN. Okay. I hear you: not now — later. *(John leaves Margaret, lopes upstairs, joins others.)* Look at *this* attic! It's like they put up a *Wild Duck* set here, insteada' on the stage. *(The sound of Nathan's TV now blends in with the chatter upstairs. Downstairs, alone, Margaret starts to clear the dinner dishes. Upstairs, the rehearsal begins.)* Okay, let's take it from Greger's first entrance.

HARRY. So, I'm putting the flute back on the shelf...

ROSIE. Are we rehearsing the English or the Original?...

JOHN. I'd like to spend a few minutes back on the Original...

HARRY. Again?

JOHN. Yuh, "again." Something the matter with "again"?

HARRY. It's just that we're getting closer and closer to the opening...

JOHN. I believe the whole point of these extra work sessions was to deepen our understanding of Ibsen's world, yes?

HARRY. I know that, John, but...

JOHN. *(Interrupting.)* Deepened understanding, Harry. That's what makes the difference between the Goods and the Greats. Now, may I...?

HARRY. Sure...sorry. *(John will now "enter" as Gregers in The Wild Duck. He will speak in pigeon-Norwegian.)*

JOHN. *Gud kvelve...*

SOPHIE. *Gud kvelve...*

JOHN. *Om forladelse—*

ROSIE. *(Realizing that it's Greger's; as Gina.)* A!

JOHN. *—er det ikke herm fotograf Ekdal bor?*

ROSIE. *Jo, det, er.*

HARRY. Me, right? Uh...oh, God, I had it perfect in the bathroom ten minutes ago...uh uh...

SOPHIE. *(Trying to throw Harry his line.)* Gregers! *Er du der alligevel? Na, sa...*

HARRY. *What?*

ROSIE. *(Prompting as well.)* ...*Er du der Alligevel?*

HARRY. *(Cutting them off.)* I know this line! I know this line!

JOHN. Come onnn, Harry, will you? The man was a *poet!* It's not

28

just *words:* there are *rhythms, music!* It's got to keep moving! *(Harry fishes in pocket, finds dog-eared paper; studies it frantically.*

HARRY. I know this line! *(Paper behind back; as a child.)* Gregers! *Er du der alligevel? Na, sa kom ind da. (Brightly.)* Okay?

JOHN. Okay, fine, let's run the whole entrance. From the top. *(Sudden switch to Gregers.) Gud kvelve...*

SOPHIE. *Gud kvelve...*

JOHN. *Om Forladelse—*

ROSIE. *A!*

JOHN. *—er det ikke her, fotograf Ekdal bor?*

ROSIE. *Jo, det er.*

HARRY. Uhhh, Gregers! *Er du der alligevel? Na, sa kom ind da.*

JOHN. *Jeg sa dig jo, at jeg vilde se op til dig.*

HARRY. *Men ikveld—? Er du gat fre selskabet?*

JOHN. *Bade fra selskabet og fra familjehjemmet. — God aften Fur Ekdal...* (Kisses Rosie's hand; bows deeply.) *Jeg ved ikke, om De kan kende mig igen?*

ROSIE. *A, jo; unge herr Wele er idde sa svaer at kende mig igen.*

JOHN. *Nej, Jeg lignier jo min mor; og hen le mindes de sagtens.* Jesus! That is just beautiful.

ROSIE. What does that mean exactly?

JOHN. That's where I say I take after my mother...

ROSIE. Oh, right...

JOHN. Because if I took after my father, then Sophie and I would look too much alike...

SOPHIE. You mean Hedvig. You said Sophie.

JOHN. No, I said Hedvig...

ROSIE. No, you didn't, John...

HARRY. You said Sophie.

SOPHIE. You did...

JOHN. What's the difference? *(There's an embarrassed pause.)*

SOPHIE. I love doing the Norwegian. English is nice, but the Norwegian is really beautiful, isn't it?

HARRY. Definitely. *(To Rosie.)* Tell John what you're doing for your inner thing.

ROSIE. I'm using Liv Ullmann.

JOHN. OOO, which movie?

ROSIE. Mostly her book about growing up...I'm almost finished. There's so much about Norway that's like Gloucester, it's eerie...

JOHN. Didn't I tell you?

ROSIE. The cold...the whole male attitude...

JOHN. These great plays are universal!

SOPHIE. Could we talk about my part? I've got to get up early for school tomorrow...

JOHN. Fine with me...

SOPHIE. Thanks, Mr. Sharp...

JOHN. You can call me "John," Sophie...

SOPHIE. It's just hard when it's your friends' father...

HARRY. It's okay, honey...

JOHN. Try.

SOPHIE. Gosh, well, *John*, can we talk about the part when Gregers says he wants to be a dog, *John?*

JOHN. Why do I say I want to be a dog?

SOPHIE. Huh?

JOHN. Not me. I mean my character, Gregers...Why would Gregers tell Hedvig he would like to be a dog?

SOPHIE. I dunno, *John*... to scare her?

JOHN. Why would Gregers want to scare Hedvig?

SOPHIE. 'Cause he's mean...

JOHN. But why would his being a dog scare Hedvig?

SOPHIE. I dunno...

JOHN. What's Hedvig's most favorite living thing next to her father?

SOPHIE. Her mother...The wild duck? *(John, Rosie, and Harry all smile.)*

JOHN. And what do hunters use to help them hunt wild ducks?

SOPHIE. A *dog?* Ohhhhhh!

JOHN. See?

SOPHIE. Gregers is really mean, isn't he?

JOHN. He's mean with a purpose. He's trying to teach Hedvig a lesson about life...

HARRY. Is anybody getting thirsty?

ROSIE. I'll go. I'm not in the next scene...

HARRY. Me, neither. We'll both go. Who wants what?

JOHN. How's the Tuborg holding out?

ROSIE. Harry just got a fresh stock.

HARRY. Charlie what'sis gave it to us for cost, 'counta' it was the Wingaersheek Players. Great guy...

ROSIE. Probably doesn't get a lot of call for Norwegian beer...

HARRY. This is possibly true...You getting the beer or am I getting the beer?

ROSIE. We're both getting the beer...

JOHN. This is digging your way to greatness as an actor...a top actor has to work a part through under the skin, through the flesh, down to the bone!

SOPHIE. So that's why you all drink Norwegian beer?

JOHN. Exactly!

SOPHIE. Sure... *(Harry and Rosie exit to stairs; they kiss. NOTE: Special light should highlight their kiss.)*

ROSIE. This is crazy, Harry. We're gonna get caught!

JOHN. *(As Gregers.)* Supposing you offered to sacrifice the wild duck for your father's sake?

SOPHIE. *(As Hedvig.)* Yes, I will try it. I will sacrifice the wild duck to prove my love for my father. *(Harry and Rosie break from the kiss. They straighten their clothing and wipe off smudged lipstick. They start downstairs. The lights shift downstairs. Margaret looks up at Rosie as Harry and Rosie enter kitchen.)*

MARGARET. How's he been acting?

ROSIE. Hmmm?

HARRY. What?

MARGARET. Harry?

ROSIE. How's he been acting?

MARGARET. In the play.

ROSIE. Oh! Great! What'cha'cooking?

MARGARET. Food. Hungry? *(Rosie opens fridge, gets Tuborg*

beer.)

HARRY. They're all thirsty. I'm hungry for a *kiss. (Harry goes to Margaret; kisses her. Rosie watches, smiling benignly. To Rosie.)* The man can't help it. He loves his wife...

MARGARET. What's that from?

HARRY. Uhhh, something...

ROSIE. *(Sings lyric.)* "I Love My Wife"...

HARRY. Hmmm?

ROSIE. The name of the show. *(Sings.)* "I Love My Wife"...

HARRY. Don't think so...

MARGARET. Don't do this for my benefit, okay? *(There is a small silence. Harry breaks it as though it never was.)*

HARRY. Who wants what? Peg? Something to drink?

MARGARET. Me? Uh uh, no thanks. I've had enough... *(Margaret looks at Rosie; smiles. Rosie returns the smile. Harry looks from one woman to another, comparing.)*

ROSIE. Cup'pa'coffee? I'll be happy to make it...

MARGARET. *(Straight at Rosie; determinately.)* I said I'd had enough, didn't I? I meant it: I've had enough. *(And with that, Margaret stands and exits the room, leaving Harry and Rosie alone.)*

ROSIE. She saw.

HARRY. She didn't.

ROSIE. She did, she saw...

HARRY. Don't be ridiculous...

ROSIE. I'm *telling* you!... *(Nathan enters the room.)*

HARRY. So, how's Earl doin', Rose?

ROSIE. *What?*

NATHAN. Anybody see the remote for the TV?

HARRY. Don't'cha' like your show?

NATHAN. Show's great. Fulla' goddamn commercials...

HARRY. Pa likes to flip during commercials...

NATHAN. Somebody took the remote out'ta the sun room... *(Looks about.)* Third time this month...

ROSIE. It's only the second of the month.

NATHAN. That's my point. *(Looks around.)* A man my age can't hop up and down every time there's a commercial. My back won't take it...My brain won't take sitting there and watchin't the goddamn commercials neither... *(Looks around.)* I'm in what they call a "bind"...TV-wise. *(Looks around.)*

ROSIE. What does it look like?

NATHAN. It's brown...not the kind with buttons...it's a squeegie-thing. You squeeze it and it makes a whoosh. Turns the TV on and off...

ROSIE. Earl says if you learn to imitate the squeegie-sound, you can turn the TV off and on by mouth...

NATHAN. I doubt that.

ROSIE. That's what he says. Earl couldn't'a made it up on his own...Too complicated an idea... *(Harry looks at Rosie. They share a smile. Nathan imitates the remote, making four or five whoosh sounds.)*

NATHAN. Whoosh! Whoooosh! Whoosh! Whooooosh! *(Falls backwards a bit.)* Dizzy! There's gotta be a less ignominious way of going than whooshing...God!...than whooshing myself to death!

MARGARET. *(Calls from offstage.)* Somethin's'a matter with the TV...It went off by itself!

NATHAN. *(Amazed.)* I'll be goddamed...Wait, I'll turn it back on for you! *(Yells his whoosh-sound again, three times.)* Whoosh! Whoooosh! Whooshhhh! *(Calls out to Margaret in other room.)* Did that fix it?

MARGARET. *(Calls from offstage, again.)* Are the lights on in there? *(Appears at door.)* The lights are on, huh? TV went off in here...

NATHAN. Musta' be'n beginnner's luck!

HARRY. Try hitting the switch on the set...

MARGARET. *(Exits; calls again from offstage.)* OK, it's on again. *(We hear TV sound again, faintly, offstage.)* It's on!

NATHAN. I'll be right there! *(To Harry and Rosie; without warning.)* Be careful, you two. Just be careful. You got more people ta' think about than just yourselves...

HARRY. What the hell are you talkin' about?

NATHAN. Children and grandparents see everything. *(He exits into sun room; slams door.)*

JOHN. *(Calls from upstairs.)* Where's my beer and my actors?

ROSIE. *(Looks worriedly at Harry then calls up to John.)* On our way! *(Rosie runs upstairs. Harry rushes to refrigerator and collects three beers; follows her up the stairs. On arrival, he hands beer to John.)*

HARRY. Here.

JOHN. Where the hell *were* you?

HARRY. Uh, talking. Downstairs. To Margaret and my father.

JOHN. Could we please get going?

HARRY. Yuh, sure, I'm ready...

SOPHIE. *(As Hedvig in The Wild Duck.)* Father! We've been waiting and waiting for you!

HARRY. Yuh, well, I said I was downstairs talking to your mother. What's the big deal? *(Sophie smiles nervously.)*

SOPHIE. What are you doing, Daddy? That was a line from the play!

ROSIE. *(As Gina in The Wild Duck; moves into Harry's arms.)* You've been gone quite a long time, Hjalmar.

HARRY. What are *you* givin' me? I was down talkin' to her mother. You were with me!

SOPHIE. Rosie *is* my mother!

HARRY. *What?*

SOPHIE. In the play, silly! You're getting totally confused!

JOHN. Okay, let's take it from the discovery of unfaithfulness.

HARRY and ROSIE. *(In anxious unison.)* What?

THE LIGHTS BLACK OUT.*
THE CURTAIN FALLS.

END OF SCENE 1.
(MUSIC IN: "Another Opening, Another Show.")**

*NOTE: At end of I-1, I suggest that the lights dim to blue *not* black, thus actors can be seen moving into position between scenes. I.H.
**See Special Note on Copyright Page.

34

Scene 2

One week later, night.

Red "no-seam" paper rolled down to create backdrop, in studio. Blowups of poster-photograph in evidence.

Nathan and Sophie are upstairs. Nathan is at work, tinting photographs. Sophie is working on her role in The Wild Duck. She might be looking for her contact lens on the floor; finding it and replacing same in her eye.

SOPHIE. It's easy to see why Hedvig got confused and killed herself instead of the duck...don't you think?

NATHAN. Who's Hedvig?

SOPHIE. My character...in the play. Weren't you listening?

NATHAN. Of course, I was listening. I just didn't remember your name was Hedvig...

SOPHIE. I've only told you maybe ten million times, Grandpa...

NATHAN. Paying attention is not my strong point... *(Smiles.)* So? You killed a duck?

SOPHIE. Gregers told Sophie that she could prove her love for her father by killing the thing in life that was dearest...

NATHAN. You mean Hedvig.

SOPHIE. What?

NATHAN. You said "Sophie." You meant "Hedvig"...You got confused...

SOPHIE. I said "Hedvig"...

NATHAN. I don't think so...

SOPHIE. Hedvig, then...

NATHAN. Killed the duck?

SOPHIE. Killed herself.

NATHAN. The little girl?

SOPHIE. She's hardly a little girl! She's fourteen!

NATHAN. She killed herself? The little girl killed herself?

SOPHIE. With this gun... *(Displays gun.)*

NATHAN. Don't point that!

SOPHIE. *(Puts gun down.)* Sorry...It's totally safe. It shoots blanks.

NATHAN. Never EVER point guns at people in real life!

SOPHIE. Sorry.

NATHAN. What the hell play are you putting on, anyway?

SOPHIE. Ibsen's *The Wild Duck*...It's been on before.

NATHAN. In Gloucester?

SOPHIE. It's a classic...I think so...

NATHAN. In Gloucester?

SOPHIE. It's been done all over the world...millions of times!

NATHAN. But, not in Gloucester...not in the last seventy - seventy - five years...I can tell you that...The little girl kills herself with a gun?

SOPHIE. She got confused. She was meant to kill the wild duck...

NATHAN. What kind of a play is this, anyhow? Not American, right?

SOPHIE. It's Norwegian.

NATHAN. To me it sounds Swedish. The highest suicide rate in the world. I've read that in the papers, many, many times. Of course, I've never read about Norwegians. Nobody has.

SOPHIE. *(Bitchily. She shows him the cover of script.)* The Ibsen play? You want to know who wrote the Ibsen play?

NATHAN. *(Imitates W.C. Fields.)* Cute. It should make me happy that your grandmother never really died...that she walks and talks on the planet Earth in the form of a fifteen year old girl. This should please me...Why doesn't it, I wonder?

SOPHIE. Who's that? Jack Benny?

NATHAN. Ooooooooooo...

SOPHIE. I didn't mean to be a bitch, Grandpa.

NATHAN. *(Still W.C. Fields.)* I suppose it's typically Norwegian...You meant to kill the duck, but, you got confused and killed my night instead...

SOPHIE. You're one of my best friends, you know...

NATHAN. See, I'm just *one* of your best friends. You're *all* of my best friends...

SOPHIE. What about Poppy?

NATHAN. No son could ever be a best friend to a father. It has to skip a generation...It's a law.

SOPHIE. What about Mama? Isn't she your best friend?

NATHAN. Your mother is my *close* friend. But you're my *best* friend...There's a small but pretty important distinction...

SOPHIE. What about the duck?

NATHAN. What *about* the duck?

SOPHIE. Don't you love the duck?

NATHAN. If I had to choose between shooting the duck and shooting myself, I would definitely...

SOPHIE. *(Leaps up; runs to duck's cage.)* Nooo! Don't listen to him...

NATHAN. ...definitely have a problem deciding...

SOPHIE. *(To duck.)* Seee? He didn't choose you...not *definitely...* *(Giggles.)*

NATHAN. There was a painter in France: Modigliani. He once said that if he passed a burning building and there was a great painting and a small cat both trapped inside, and if he only had time to save one or the other, he would choose the cat...to save. He would let the great painting burn.

SOPHIE. Oh, me, too, definitely...

NATHAN. I wish I knew what I would do...

SOPHIE. Don't you like cats, Grandpa?

NATHAN. That's not *it.*

SOPHIE. What's *it?*

NATHAN. I wish I knew. The difficult thing for me is deciding, period. I hate to conclude anything about anything. Seems to me that there's a tremendous difference between what *is* and what *could be.* It's a shame to settle for *what is.* I mean, well, it makes less of life, doesn't it? Go study yo'r Algebra. You've got a test tomorrow.

SOPHIE. I've got to study lines, Grandpa. Algebra's just numbers: plays are *life!*

NATHAN. There's safety in numbers. *(The lights crossfade to downstairs. John enters through the back door. John opens refrigerator and looks for a beer, finds one and opens it. The light from the refrigerator illuminates the entire kitchen. Margaret enters through the front door, carrying a bag of groceries. She enters the room, switches on the lights, John spins around and faces her. Both are startled.)*

MARGARET. Ohhh!

JOHN. You startled me.

MARGARET. I was...out.

JOHN. I'm early...

MARGARET. You're working here again tonight?

JOHN. Working here in a real photographic studio on a play that's set in a photographic studio, makes things seem, I dunno...*real.* *(Crossfade back to Sophie and Nathan upstairs.)*

NATHAN. You have to be really careful when you're doing plays not to forget who you really are. Plays are dangerous. Sometimes, people get too caught up in the play they're doing.

SOPHIE. Oh, I know. I'm *totally* caught up. It's all I think about...

NATHAN. When your grandmother was acting in a play, our lives always changed. I remember when she was playin' in *The King and I,* life wasn't worth living! Every time I stood up, she stood up *higher. (Crossfade back to Margaret and John downstairs.)*

JOHN. The extra rehearsal's good for Harry, too. He's a little slow with his lines...

MARGARET. What time you startin'?

JOHN. Seven. I'm a little early... *(Smiles.)* Harry's pickin' up Rosie. I let myself in. The back door was open...

MARGARET. Oh.

JOHN. Just us down here, I guess, huh? *(There is a shared stare. Margaret starts to speak, thinks better of it. John walks to her; kisses her.)* Margaret, I...

MARGARET. *(Pulls back from him; shocked.)* Please, Jack, don't...

JOHN. It's alright...

MARGARET. It's not alright! I can't handle this, Jack.

JOHN. I still have strong feelings for you, Peggy...

MARGARET. Please *don't!* I just can't...I won't.

JOHN. I never stopped...

MARGARET. You never stopped *what?*

JOHN. ...*loving* you! Since the year of *Our Town*...if my father had cast me instead of Harry, you would have been married to me probably, right?

MARGARET. We don't know that!

JOHN. I know it!

MARGARET. *Our Town* was fifteen years ago, Jack, for God's sake! A good couple of boats have passed under the cut-bridge since Grovers Corners.

JOHN. Peggy... *(Tries to kiss her. She resists.)* Peggy...

MARGARET. Jack, for God's sake...*stop it!* (She exits into sun room; slams door. John stands alone in the kitchen, drinking beer, sadly. Crossfade back to Nathan and Sophie upstairs.)

SOPHIE. Why did Grandma make you promise to quit acting?

NATHAN. 'Cause I could never stick to the lines. I always tried to make them funny. Seems to me an audience deserves a couple of giggles on their night out. If you can't give 'em a lousy couple of giggles, why take their money and their time?

SOPHIE. Mr. Sharp's always trying to improve *The Wild Duck*, too. He says the play got bad reviews 'cause directors and actors have been doing it all backwards...trying to make a comedy out of a very serious play.

NATHAN. Who would've guessed John Sharp would've known so much...

SOPHIE. Oh, he's really, really smart, Grandpa...

NATHAN. So was his father. He had everybody doing *Julius Caesar* as a "war for control of the Gloucester waterfront." Brutus was a lobsterman...Cassius was a lumper. Come to think of it, John

39

Sharp's father got quite a lot of comedy out of *Julius Caesar*. Mixing tragedy and comedy must just be an in their blood kind of thing. Algebra! *(Sophie exits into her bedroom. Crossfade back to Margaret and John downstairs. Margaret reenters from sun room.)*

JOHN. Peggy, please, it's alright...

MARGARET. How come you keep saying "It's alright"? What's alright? Making out in my kitchen with my father-in-law and daughter upstairs? Is that what's alright? How come? How come? *(John tries to kiss her again.)* What is *with* you?

JOHN. I want to tell you something, Marg...Please, it's really important. Something I've never told anybody.

MARGARET. There are other people in the house, you know...

JOHN. Nobody knows where I went and what I did when I was gone five years...

MARGARET. In Alaska?

JOHN. Hmmm?

MARGARET. When you went to Alaska?

JOHN. I never went to Alaska.

MARGARET. Everybody said you did. That's what it said in the paper...

JOHN. That's my point.

MARGARET. What's your point?

JOHN. I was in Milford, New Hampshire.

MARGARET. When?

JOHN. The five years I was out'ta town.

MARGARET. Then how come the paper said Alaska?

JOHN. Margaret, I am trying to confide in you!

MARGARET. Why?

JOHN. Because, you mean something to me. Please. Listen to me

MARGARET. I'm listening. *(She sits down at kitchen table.)*

JOHN. I couldn't sit across the table from Allison every night, knowing that I was living a deception...

MARGARET. So you moved to Milford, New Hampshire?

JOHN. Please!

MARGARET. Sorry.

JOHN. One day — cold as a son of a bitch — I'm walkin' on Good Harbor Beach, watching ducks leavin' town, thinkin' about wint'ah comin' on...and I started to envy the ducks. Honest ta' Christ. And I took off. Just like that.

MARGARET. Up?

JOHN. What?

MARGARET. Like the ducks? Allison probably shoulda' tagged your foot...

JOHN. *(Really annoyed.)* What are you talking about?

MARGARET. Sorry.

JOHN. I left town for five years, Margaret, five years. Do you have any idea how much courage that takes: to leave from Allison, two twins, Gloucester, my mother and all my aunts and uncles and cousins, the Players, lifelong friends, work, all that...

MARGARET. I guess.

JOHN. I *know.*

MARGARET. So, why'd you pick Milford, New Hampshire?

JOHN. That's what I'm leadin' up to. I got out this map of the world and I put it on the wall down the cellar...and I got out one dart*...

MARGARET. I thought you just took off from Good Harbor Beach?

JOHN. I had'da pack, didn't I? *(Pauses; then quietly.)* I wanted one last look, too. Just in case I was makin' a mistake...

MARGARET. And you knew you weren't, when you looked at Allison and the twins?

JOHN. Nobody was home. Allison was down Liberty Tree Mall with her mother. The twins were stayin' overnight over the Websters. Allison left a note sayin' all that, and that there was a casserole for me to heat up when I got hungry... *(Pauses; then, resolutely.)* After that, I had no doubt...

MARGARET. Jesus! What was in the casserole?

JOHN. What's this?

MARGARET. So, you packed?

JOHN. First I threw the dart 'case I hit a hot place or a cold

*NOTE: Pronounced "dahht."

41

place...you know...Africa, or, say...

MARGARET. Alaska...

JOHN. Exactly. *(Pauses.)* I hit Milford.

MARGARET. Are you kidding me?

JOHN. I know! It was the most amazing thing. It's a huge fucking map, too! Takes up the better part of a whole sheet of wallboard. Used'ta be up on the twins' wall, till they wanted TV stars and somesuch, so I put it down cellar...

MARGARET. How far back were you standing?

JOHN. Regulation distance...

MARGARET. I thought you used to be really good at darts.

JOHN. That's my point. I shoulda' b'en able ta' hit any of the world's great places: Paris, Rome, you name it. Some things are *fated.* The Greeks got at that in those plays. It was like some savage God got ahold of my dart...

MARGARET. I would've thrown another dart...

JOHN. I thought of that, but then there woulda' be'n two different places...I felt I was being sent to Milford, New Hampshire, so I went...I got this job, doin' stuff...subsistence kind of thing...

MARGARET. For five years? *(John looks up; annoyed, again. She goes on.)* Five years is a long time to sit around...

JOHN. I wasn't exactly sitting around... *(Margaret nods.)* They've got this theatre up in Milford...

MARGARET. Uh-huh.

JOHN. They do some really heady stuff, sometimes, too... *(Pauses.)* That's how I saw *The Wild Duck*... *(Proudly.)* I saw Ibsen's *The Wild Duck* thirteen times, all the way through, and it changed my life, Marg...

MARGARET. Did it?

JOHN. It's all about how people have to get rid of deception in their lives...how they have to be totally realistic and totally honest if they're ever going to be totally happy. Ibsen has this thing he's against called "The Saving Lie"...the way people try to not hurt each other's feelings by telling a little saving lie here and another little saving lie there...and sooner or later it all accumulates and the people's lives are like *huge lies*...their whole lives!

MARGARET. That's what *The Wild Duck* is about?

JOHN. I know this play inside out!

MARGARET. That's what they tell me.

JOHN. I went every night. Matinees, too. After the show closed, I got the book out of the library and I read it over and over and over until I knew what I'd been waiting for...till I knew what my next move was... *(Margaret looks up at John, silently, waiting. John savors the moment, makes the best of it.)* I knew that I had to come home — here — to Gloucester...to Allison and the children...to you and Sophie...I knew that I had to put on *The Wild Duck.* I knew that I had to direct it myself and play the lead role myself... *(Nathan is eavesdropping at top of stairs.)*

MARGARET. I thought Sophie was the lead...

JOHN. She plays the kid.

MARGARET. How about Harry? He's got a lot of lines...

JOHN. Gregers is the lead. Gregers carries the message of the play...People must give up all deception, be totally realistic and truthful...give up "the saving lie," totally. *(John moves to Margaret and tries to hug her. He gathers her close to him.)* Life is so different when you have a reason...a purpose...when you know the real truth. Give me the real truth. Tell me what you really think of me, Marg, please? Be totally honest with me. Please. I can take it. *(There is a small pause.)*

MARGARET. I think you're about the weirdest dork on the planet Earth.

JOHN. See? That would've hurt most guys. But, now I know the truth, so I can work on changing things around...at getting you to change your truth...at getting you to remember the wonderful truth that once was... *(Nathan enters from upstairs; Margaret quickly moves towards dining room.)*

NATHAN. *(To John, with hostility.)* Som'pin' particular you're afta'?

JOHN. We were just rehearsing, that's all!

NATHAN. I didn't hear you come in...

JOHN. I just got here...

MARGARET. He let himself in...

JOHN. The back door was open...

NATHAN. I didn't hear any car...

JOHN. I walked...

NATHAN. In the snow?

JOHN. I wanted to think...

NATHAN. In the snow?

JOHN. Well, sure...It's less than a mile.

NATHAN. Suit yourself... *(Pauses; looks at Margaret.)* You okay?

MARGARET. I dunno. Why? *(We hear the sound of a car turning into the driveway; stopping.)*

JOHN. That must be them. *(The sound of a car door closing. Then another.)*

MARGARET. Yes. *(John and Margaret stand facing each other, silently. Sophie calls down from upstairs.)*

SOPHIE. Is that them? You hear a car pull up?

MARGARET. *(Calls upstairs.)* That's them, yes...

SOPHIE. *(Looks down from balcony-overhang.)* Hi, Mr. Sharp!

JOHN. Hello, Miss Budd.

SOPHIE. I'll be right back! I just have to finish putting up my hair, *John. (Exits.)*

NATHAN. *(To John.)* Who picked this play, anyhow?

JOHN. *The Wild Duck?* The committee...

NATHAN. It's a little weird for the Wingaersheek Players, don't you think?

JOHN. It's a classic.

NATHAN. Not around these parts...

JOHN. Henrik Ibsen.

NATHAN. He ain't local, is he?

JOHN. He's dead.

NATHAN. Buried local?

JOHN. He was Norwegian...

NATHAN. That's what I heard.

JOHN. A lot'ta people in town, not just in the Wingaersheek Players, neither, think Ibsen should be done in Gloucester...

NATHAN. And that influenced you in choosing?

JOHN. You gotta try to please people with the plays you do...

NATHAN. What certain people are you trying to please? How many goddamn Norwegians you think we got livin' in Gloucester, anyway? *(Harry enters with Rosie; Both wearing heavy winter coats, gloves, hats and scarves. They are holding hands. Both are extremely nervous. Rosie's head is down. Harry is sweating. John doesn't notice at first that they are holding hands.)*

JOHN. What the hell kept you?

HARRY. Rosie and I need to talk with Peg, alone...

NATHAN. What are you doing, Harry?

HARRY. Alone, Pa...

JOHN. I... *(Sees them holding hands.)* I'll go inta the front room...or should I wait in my house? I wouldn't mind goin' home and just waitin' for you ta' call me.

ROSIE. *(A whisper.)* Just wait a minute in there, Jack...

NATHAN. What the hell do you think you're *doing?*

MARGARET. I think you better go in the other room, Nathan...

NATHAN. This is my house, too. I hang my goddamn hat here, too, ya know. This is "Home Sweet Home" for me, too. Leggo of her hand, Harold.

HARRY. Stay out'ta this, Pa. I know what I'm doing...

NATHAN. *(To Rosie.)* You out'ta your mind, sistah? Comin' inta somebody else's house, carryin' on? This is a family, you know...

HARRY. *Pa, damn you, butt out!*

NATHAN. Everybody seen it going on, ya know? *Everybody!* You make it so nobody can pretend otherwise. You make it so people gotta see *just what is,* period.

MARGARET. Seen what, Pa? Harry? Seen what? Somebody better tell me what's goin' on here, huh?

JOHN. Uhhh, I'll just hop inta the TV room. Comin' in, Mr. Budd?

HARRY. Get in there, damn you! Go! *(There is a pause, as Father and Son stare at one another.)*

45

NATHAN. I'll be just inside, Margaret, if you want me... *(To Harry.)* You shame me. *(Nathan and John exit. Margaret faces Harry.)*

MARGARET. Seen what, Harry? What's everybody seen?

HARRY. Peg, you must know...

MARGARET. I must know what?

HARRY. Peg...

ROSIE. Harry and I have be'n seein' each other, Peg.

MARGARET. "Seein' each other"?

ROSIE. Well, yuh...we have.

MARGARET. What does that mean? Like extra rehearsals kind of thing?

HARRY. Besides that. We see each other in real life, too.

MARGARET. You mean like a *couple?*

HARRY. For a long time now, Peg...

MARGARET. How long?

HARRY. Three years. Ever since the year of *Who's Afraid Of Virginia Woolf?*

MARGARET. Oh. *(There is a long wordless pause. Margaret turns, walks to the wall, leans against wall, turns and faces Harry and Rosie. Rosie takes a step toward Margaret, thinks better of it, looks at Harry, who takes a step toward Margaret, thinks better of it; stops. Harry and Rosie look at one another and then look down. All three hold their places another full beat, wordlessly. Sophie bounds down the stairs, happily. On hearing her voice, Harry drops his hold on Rosie's hand, instantly.)*

SOPHIE. Where the hell *were* you guys, anyhow? I thought we were gonna start at 7:00... *(Goes to Rosie; hugs her, kisses her.)* Hiii, Rosie. You sad about something? *(Suddenly.)* What's the matter?

ROSIE. Come with me, into the TV room. John's in there...

SOPHIE. Why?

ROSIE. John's in there. We can go over lines...

SOPHIE. What's the matter?

ROSIE. Your father needs to talk with your mom, just the two of them...

SOPHIE. Why? What's the matter?

MARGARET. Just...just give us a couple of minutes...

HARRY. Maybe she should stay. We've got no secrets... *(Margaret answers without hesitation.)*

MARGARET. No. *(To Sophie.)* Go in the other room with your grandfather...

SOPHIE. I don't think I want to...

MARGARET. Please.

SOPHIE. I don't like this. *(Sophie exits; Rosie starts off. Margaret stops her.)*

MARGARET. No! You stay...

HARRY. Margaret...

MARGARET. *(As powerfully as might Martha [Who's Afraid of Virginia Woolf] speak these words.)* She stays!

ROSIE. It's okay. I'll stay...

MARGARET. So?

HARRY. This is difficult.

MARGARET. Anything I can do to help out?...I'd like to make it easier for you guys, if I can...

ROSIE. *(Frightened; stutters.)* We didn't want to start...

MARGARET. *(Imitates Rosie's stutter.)* Somebody forced you?

ROSIE. We held off for a long time...

HARRY. All during the year of *Death of a Salesman* and the year of *Auntie Mame*...

MARGARET. You were...a couple?

ROSIE. We held off...

HARRY. We didn't even smile at each other till the year of *The Fantastiks*...

MARGARET. *The Fantastiks?*...

HARRY. The musical...

MARGARET. I know it's a fucking musical! *(She exits through kitchen door outside.)*

ROSIE. *(Calls out the door.)* Margie! *(Pronounced MAH-GEE. Margaret reenters from front door; shivers.)* I'm sorry, Margie. I really am.

MARGARET. Oh, well, sure you're sorry. *(Pause.)* Does Earl know?

47

ROSIE. Not yet.

MARGARET. *(Offers kitchen wall-phone.)* Don't you think we should ring him up...get him over here?

ROSIE. *(Grabs phone; hangs it up.)* Not yet!

MARGARET. Just me and Sophie? We're the only ones who're s'pose'ta know about this?

ROSIE. We'll tell Earl...

HARRY. We wanted to tell you first...

MARGARET. Really? Why?

HARRY. Because you're my wife. Because we both...care about you.

MARGARET. I...feel...cold.

HARRY. Neither of us is proud about this, Peg. We're both pretty sorry and ashamed...

MARGARET. Right.

ROSIE. We just wanted to stop the lying.

MARGARET. Together?

ROSIE. Hmmm?

MARGARET. *(Obscene clapping geture supports thought.)* The lying together: you and Harold...him on top...that kind of thing? Is that what you're stopping?

ROSIE. I meant the deception...the accumulation of ten million saving lies...

HARRY. It's driving us both crazy...We can't sleep...

MARGARET. Wait till Earl finds out. He'll put you both to sleep...

ROSIE. I don't think Earl's gonna mind much...

MARGARET. You getting married, or what? *(A pause, both Harry and Rosie look up.)* To each other, you and the Boss...You leave Earl, he leaves me, his daughter, his father... *(Smiles.)* That what you two are plannin'?

HARRY. I would never...

ROSIE. Uh uh. Not at all...

MARGARET. You're not leaving? You're staying?

HARRY. We wanted to stop the deception, that's all.

MARGARET. What the hell do *you* know about deception?

HARRY. What'da you mean?

MARGARET. *(Smugly; punches her palm four times.)* That's for me to know and you to find out...What'daya' think Earl's gonna' say, Rosie?

ROSIE. He'll be...upset.

MARGARET. *(Sits; makes pronouncement.)* Earl's be'n sleepin' with Janice Dodge ever since high school. I s'pose you know that, huh?

ROSIE. Not, uh, definitely. I don't know that definitely.

HARRY. C'mon, Peg, huh?

MARGARET. Oh, it's definite, alright. Janice told me herself, many times. We go to the same coiffure...We very often sit under the dryers, side by side, me and Janice Dodge...She says it's just a physical thing, Earl and her. She thinks Earl is a wicked dunce, but, you know, what'd she say?...*beastial*...kinda' like some kinda', you know...*beast.* *(Smiles; speaks with more pronounced accent.)* They sta'hted in senior year...and never stopped.

ROSIE. *(She offers her palms.)* If you have to, Ma'hg, I... understand.

MARGARET. Good. *(There is another long wordless pause. Harry breaks it. He tries to get up the stairs, gracefully.)*

HARRY. Well. We should get the others, huh. It's getting late.

MARGARET. What's this?

HARRY. Two weeks till opening, that's all...

MARGARET. You're gonna rehearse?

HARRY. Upstairs. If that's alright.

MARGARET. I... *(Starts to speak; stops herself. She laughs, instead. Harry and Rosie stand watching her laugh. Harry joins in the laughter. Then Rosie joins in. Margaret stops laughing, looks at them both, contemptuously. Sensing her stare, they both stop laughing, as well. Martha, again.)* Whose idea was this?...You're both tellin' me...straight out...face-to-face? Whose idea was it? *(John reenters from other room, silently. He stares from one to the other, proudly.)*

JOHN. *(Quietly, pretentiously; profoundly: He is sensae.)* I'll bet that you all feel much better. *(Pauses.)* If you don't, you're going to feel a *lot* better, and soon, too. *(Pauses.)* No doubt about it.

49

MARGARET. Oh.

HARRY. It's better this way, Peg. It really is...

JOHN. When I was up in New Hampshire all that time, on my own, just thinking about people...about me and Allison...about marriage, about the *idea* of marriage I had a realization, like a lightning bolt hit: the million little saving lies; the deceptions. That's what dries a marriage out; kills it. *(Pauses.)* Turns people from being kind to being mean.

ROSIE. Love to hate...

JOHN. The truth is easier... *(Smiles.)* We're all just people...

HARRY. We don't do anything that other people don't do...

JOHN. That's not it, exactly, but, it's close...

MARGARET. You're planning to rehearse upstairs tonight? Upstairs? The buncha'ya's?

JOHN. We have a play to rehearse. We put on plays. It's who we are. It's what we do.

ROSIE. It's who we are. It's what we do. *(Pauses.)* If we didn't put on plays, nobody would...Whole winters would go by with no theatrical entertainment...Putting on plays is a great thing. It's kept all us friends together, hasn't it? *(Margaret looks at a slightly embarrassed Harry.)*

MARGARET. This is a lunatic. This is Claire de Lune. *(Sophie bursts into dining room from TV room. Nathan follows; worried.)*

SOPHIE. Something awful's happened, hasn't it?

MARGARET. *(To Nathan.)* What'd you tell her?

NATHAN. *(Shows palms to Margaret. He mouths a word, behind Sophie's back.)* Nothin'.

MARGARET. *(To John, Harry and Rosie.)* Could we hold off killing her deception for another couple'a days? *(Harry looks at his wife; confused.)* I need some time to digest this... *(Margaret makes eye contact with Harry.)* Could we just hold off another couple'a days? Please, Harry... *(She hold back her tears. Harry flashes a worried look at John and then at Rosie, who nods affirmatively.)*

HARRY. Sure. 'Course... *(Sophie runs to Margaret; hugs her.)*

SOPHIE. Are you sick? Is that it, Mama? Is that what everybody's hiding from me?

MARGARET. Nooo.

SOPHIE. God, I got scared. Mary-Ellen Boley's mother is wicked awful sick. Everybody knows...

JOHN. Be patient, Hedvig...trust the people you love. *(Rosie is deeply moved by these words. Harry is embarrassed again. Margaret and Harry glance at each other. A moment.)*

ROSIE. Ohh. *(Sophie looks at John; smiles.)*

SOPHIE. *(Brightly.)* Are we gonna' rehearse? *(There is a pause. Harry looks at Margaret.)*

HARRY. Peg?

MARGARET. *(After a pause; shrugs.)* Sure.

SOPHIE. *(Enormously relieved.)* Could we start with Act Four? I have it all down perfect!

JOHN. *(Smiles at Sophie, lovingly.)* Sure. We'll start at the top of Act Four. Is Henrik ready?

SOPHIE. I'll get him, John... *(Stops; to Margaret.)* We named the duck "Henrik," after the man who wrote the play. It was John's idea.

JOHN. Seemed obvious.

MARGARET. *(Ironically.)* Wicked clever...

SOPHIE. *(Joyously relieved.)* I'll get Henrik in two shakes... *(Starts up staircase.)* Hurry up, you guys. I've got school tomorrow! *(Runs upstairs; appears at top.)* Henrik! Get ready to rehearse! *(There is a pause, as John turns from following Sophie with his eyes, to face Margaret; silently, smiles. Margaret stares at John, directly. John turns, smiles at Rosie and Harry.)*

JOHN. We'd better head up, huh? We've got work to do.

ROSIE. Just give me a minute...

JOHN. I'll be up with Soph, waiting,... *(Exits upstairs; strokes Harry as he passes him.)*

HARRY. Uh, I'll be right up... *(Rosie goes to Margaret; takes her to one side, confidentially.)*

ROSIE. I'm sorry, Marg. I really am...

MARGARET. Are you?

ROSIE. I'm about as sorry as anyone can be... *(Sophie calls from the top of the stairs.)*

SOPHIE. C'mon, you guys! We're ready!

ROSIE. Coming! *(To Margaret.)* I'd better go up...

MARGARET. Rosie! *(Rosie looks at Margaret.)* What do you see in Harry? *(There is a pause. Harry and Nathan both look away, but listen intently, both facing front.)*

ROSIE. Honest to God?

MARGARET. Honest to God.

ROSIE. *(She looks at Harry who is standing by the stairs.)* About ninety pounds less than Earl. *(Pause.)* And he never hits me. *(Rosie goes upstairs, joining John and Sophie. Harry watches Rosie exit and than stares at Margaret. Upstairs, rehearsal begins, in whispers. Downstairs, Margaret turns toward stove and Harry approaches her. He stands directly behind her and speaks gently.)*

HARRY. *(Softly; sincerely.)* I was scared stiff. *(Pauses.)* I didn't know how you'd take it... *(Pauses.)* I thought our marriage was wrecked, Peg. I really did... *(Pauses.)* All the time I was lyin', I... *(Pauses.)* Now that I found the courage to talk...to tell you exactly what gives, well... *(Smiles.)* I feel like I did when we were first married. Honest to God. *(Softly.)* I love you, Peg... *(Harry leans in to kiss Margaret. Without warning, Margaret slaps Harry. It is not at all a girlish slap. It is a fabulous, resounding wallop that produces a full cracking sound. Harry reels backwards, slamming against the fridge. He grabs ahold for ballast. There is a stunned silence.)* I'd better head on up. *(Upstairs, John, Rosie and Sophie run through the lines that start Act Four of Ibsen's The Wild Duck, arriving at the cue for Hjalmar's entrance, just as Harry's foot hits the bottom step.)*

ROSIE. *(As Gina.)* Don't worry like that. He's coming...

SOPHIE. *(As Hedvig.)* Oh, I wish so he'd hurry up. Everything seems so strange now...

ROSIE. *(As Gina.)* Here he is! *(Harry reaches the point at the top of the staircase at which he is visible to the audience. Sophie runs to him; hugs him.)*

SOPHIE. *(As Hedvig.)* Father, you're here! We've been waiting and waiting and waiting for you!

HARRY. *(As Hjalmar, in The Wild Duck.)* I'm home...

ROSIE. *(As Gina.)* You've been out for a long time, Hjalmar...

HARRY. *(Sadly; as Hjalmar.)* Yes, I guess I have...a long time. Hedvig...Gina...I'm home now. *(Harry embraces Rosie and Sophie, upstairs. The action pauses, upstairs. Downstairs, Margaret is sobbing. The forgotten Nathan leaves his place silently staring in from the threshold to the sunroom [TV room], goes to Margaret, and hugs her.)*

MARGARET. *(Sobbing.)* I just don't know what to do, Pa. I just don't know what to do.

NATHAN. I think we'd better read the play. *(Margaret sobs in Nathan's arms. The lights fade. MUSIC IN: "Soon it's gonna rain..."* * etc.)*

THE CURTAIN FALLS.

END OF ACT I.

*See Special Note on Copyright Page.

ACT II
Scene 1

Night, one week later. Dark blue "no-seam" pulled down now as backdrop in studio, upstairs. Finished posters for The Wild Duck, featuring Harry's photograph, are in evidence. Margaret sits at table in dining room preparing the evening meal. Harry is doing his exercises. He's doing push-ups with his hands on two chairs and his feet on the stairs. He does thirty-five push-ups.

HARRY. You must have known *something,* Peg.

MARGARET. I heard some giggling upstairs a couple of times when I came home from the shop early, yuh...

HARRY. Oh, God, *really?*

MARGARET. Yuh, well, really.

HARRY. So, what did you do?

MARGARET. I went out again. Took a walk.

HARRY. God! When was that?

MARGARET. *(Annoyed by Harry's delight.)* I don't know...a couple of weeks ago. Are you enjoying this?

HARRY. God, no! *(Pause.)* Look, I know how hard this is for you. But, it's not like I'm having all the fun and you're not.

MARGARET. You're not having fun? Oh my gosh. Oh my goodness...

HARRY. Come on, Peg. Like John says, this kind of thing takes time. When all the lies are gone there's only truth to face...and truth hurts at first. John thinks this painful part...will pass in less than a week.

MARGARET. He's really got this down to a science, doesn't he?

HARRY. He's always looking for deception...and finding it. It's kinda'...his thing.

MARGARET. Like pigs with truffles.

HARRY. I love a smart remark!

MARGARET. Wouldn't think I was capable of smart remarks. Not like you or Rosie or John. Not like you show business personalities...

HARRY. He's okay. He's only tryin' ta' help out.

MARGARET. I can see that.

HARRY. He's been through it himself...

MARGARET. Through what?

HARRY. A bad marriage. Like us.

MARGARET. 'S' that what we've been through?

HARRY. I think you know what I mean...We're havin' our troubles same as everybody else. Some people have 'em early on, some even get divorced. Ours were just late comin', that's all...Look at John and Allison: split up for five years and all...John, up in New Hampshire, alone, the way he was, thinkin' all the time. John's deep.

MARGARET. So's Niles Pond.

HARRY. Marvelous. I'm gonna' tell you something. As far as I'm concerned, he's the one who saved our marriage.

MARGARET. John?

HARRY. Right.

MARGARET. John Sharp?

HARRY. John Sharp...

MARGARET. Saved our marriage?

HARRY. That's the way I see it. I don't think we'd be married if not for John Sharp. *(Margaret laughs. Nathan enters from the sun room [TV room]. Stares.)* What's so funny? What's so goddamn funny?

MARGARET. I think you're right. I really do. *(Margaret laughs again.)*

HARRY. I don't like this. *(Harry is suddenly aware of his father in the room.)* Yuh, what?

NATHAN. I can't remember what I came in here for. *(Pauses, thinks, still can't remember.)* Hmmm. *(Shrugs; exits back into sun room.)*

HARRY. I think he's taking all this a little harder than he ought'ta, don't you?

MARGARET. I dunno. He's your father. Mine's dead. If mine were alive, he'd probably take it pretty hard, too. He'd probably open up yo'r stomach with a clammin' knife...

HARRY. I just wanna' say one thing here...

MARGARET. Oh, yuh? What?

HARRY. I know plenty'a guys have walked out on their families, left 'em high and dry. I know plenty, you know plenty. I ain't doing that. Nothing *like* that. I got family responsibilities and I'm sticking by them.

MARGARET. That's the one thing you've got to say?

HARRY. Yuh.

MARGARET. Okay.

HARRY. *(After a pause.)* Swiggy Carlson: he left Marian. Sally Morella: he left Carmella. Kermie Ferguson left what'shername...

MARGARET. Yuh, so?

HARRY. Yuh, so, am I leaving you in the lurch and causing those kinda' bullshit problems?

MARGARET. It's true. You're not the worst. The guy up Top of the Harbor apartments who chopped up his mother and tried to stuff her down the garbage disposal...he was worse. It's true...

HARRY. You married me out of your own free will. Nobody forced you. You were mature.

MARGARET. Nineteen is not mature. Horny, maybe, but certainly not mature. *(Harry "shhhhhhushes" her; checks to see that Sophie can't overhear.)*

HARRY. You know what I mean.

MARGARET. I always know what you mean. That's the trouble!

HARRY. Shit!

MARGARET. What?

HARRY. Here it is, ha'pahst eight, pitch-black out, about two above zero, nothin' doin' ten towns around, you *at* me...It's like

56

*prison*here! I'm trapped!

MARGARET. Why don't you watch televison?

HARRY. I don't wanna' watch television...He's watching his homo-poet show again...

MARGARET. Read something.

HARRY. Don't tell me what to do, okay? *(He walks in a circle.)* I know this must sound strange to you, but, as trapped as I feel, I feel *freer*...because I told you the truth.

MARGARET. No matter how much it hurts *me?*

HARRY. The truth doesn't hurt you, Margaret. It's lies and deception that hurts you. The truth just *is*. It's like this table, or your stove there: *facts*...unalterable facts.

MARGARET. It's a small point, but it's not "my" stove, it's *our* stove.

HARRY. Fine.

MARGARET. Okay. How about *me,* Harry? Can I tell *you* the truth?

HARRY. Anything. *(Shows his palms.)* Anything. *(Smiles.)* I would welcome it.

MARGARET. *(After a pause.)* I wish you were dead, Harry. It would be a lot easier for me, and for Soph...and probably for your father, too. *(Puts food back in fridge.)* I'm goin' to bed. *(Goes to staircase.)* Turn out the lights before you go out. The light shines into the bedroom and I can see the clock while I'm layin' there, not sleeping. I hate to know how late it is...two, three, four... *(Pauses.)* I really hate it.

HARRY. *(Suddenly.)* She's *somebody*, Margaret. Can't you see that? Rosie's *somebody*.

MARGARET. Why don't you call Earl up and ask him if Rosie can come out and play?

HARRY. Don't. Okay? Just don't. *(Pauses.)* I'm trying to explain something to you, that's all... *(Pauses; new solicitous tone.)* Rosemary Bennedetto was always special to me. Even back when we were seven, I kinda' had a thing for her. Don't forget, we did a play together then. When we were just seven years old.

MARGARET. "The Seven Year Old Itch"?

57

HARRY. When we were in *Julius Caesar* together, we had to change in the same dressing room. I remember staring at her, all the way back then...

MARGARET. Why are you telling me this?

HARRY. Because I want you to understand...

MARGARET. And you figure I don't?

HARRY. Don't what?

MARGARET. Don't understand?

HARRY. Rosemary and I were in five different plays together, before we were, what, eleven...twelve... *(Thinks.) Julius Caesar, Our Miss Brooks, Brigadoon...The Playboy of the Western World...The Importance of Being Earnest.* We were *all* in that one...

MARGARET. Yes.

HARRY. You, me, Rosie, Earl, Jr. ...My *father* even. He took the stills and played...the *butler*... *(Smiles; happily.)* We go back some, don't we, Peg?

MARGARET. It's not the goin' back that worries me, Harry. It's the goin' forward. Worse yet, it's the standin' still.

HARRY. A lot of people have open marriages. We're not exactly the inventors...

MARGARET. Excuse me? What?

HARRY. That's all that's goin' on here. There's never be'n any need to make such a big deal out'ta this. You read about it all the goddamn time, really...

MARGARET. I don't.

HARRY. What?

MARGARET. Read about it. I read my *Gloucester Times* and my *Boston Globe* and my *Gourmet* and *Better Homes and Gardens* and I read some pretty weird goin's-on, I do admit, but, never, not even once, in my whole life, have I read about shit like you're tryin' ta' pull on this family, Harold. And that is a God's-honest-no-bullshit-motherfucking *fact!*

HARRY. Will you kindly watch your tongue?

MARGARET. *(Tries, literally, to watch her tongue.)* Sorry, but my face just don't seem to be built that way.

HARRY. My own mother cheated on my own father: total deception that should've been brought out in the open...

MARGARET. *Shhh!*

HARRY. *(Whispering.)* Well, it's a fact.

MARGARET. *(Whispering.)* He doesn't know!

HARRY. *(Whispering.)* He knows. He just doesn't let it *sink in.*

MARGARET. *(Whispering.)* And that's what you call an *open marriage*, you dumb shit?

HARRY. Could you curb your language?

MARGARET. You mean like my dog? Like my old cocker?

HARRY. Exactly! You got it! Exactly like your old cocker!

MARGARET. Fuck you.

HARRY. Okay, I've had enough.

MARGARET. Great.

HARRY. I'm goin' out. *(Exits to front hall.)*

MARGARET. Great. *(Harry returns after pause with coat.)*

HARRY. You'll be alone.

MARGARET. Fine.

HARRY. Maybe I won't come back tonight.

MARGARET. Okay.

HARRY. How come you're acting like this?

MARGARET. Acting like what?

HARRY. Bitchy, cold, heartless.

MARGARET. Maybe it's just that time of the month...

HARRY. Come *oonnn*, Peg...

MARGARET. Maybe it's just that time of the *life...*

HARRY. We were all in that, too...

MARGARET. What?

HARRY. *The Time of Your Life...*you, me, Earl Jr., Rosie, Mama...-John, too... *(Whispers.)* John's father, Big John Sharp...That was the first time I knew for sure about my mother and him...they were in the rehearsal room together. I wanted a dime for a candy bar, I remember that. The door was stuck and I heaved my shoulder into it and it flew goddamn wide open, like a curtain goin' up...and there they were. I thought they were fighting. Honest ta'God. 'Course, they weren't. Opposite. Big clinch. Passionate.

MARGARET. *(Motions to sun room. She protects Nathan from hear-*

59

ing.) Shhhh. *(Harry is obviously in good spirits again. He goes to sun room door, closes same, after peeking in and smiling a greeting.)*

NATHAN. *(Offstage; he has been awakened.)* Whattt? Jesus, Harold, I was sleeping'!

HARRY. *(To Nathan.)* Sorry. Just shuttin' it up. Peg and I are havin' a private talk... *(Harry closes door; turns to face Margaret.)* So... *(Tries to remember; recapture mood. He stands with his hands in fists by his ears, much like an actor in rehearsal. Finally, he remembers: he has the mood. He speaks, not at all unhappily.)* They were really goin' at it, like they were in a movie or somesuch. Mama yelled at me in a kind of a hoarse, throaty whisper: "What the hell do you want, Harold?" *(Answers; child's voice.)* A dime, Mama... *(His own voice, again; softly.)* Then she started to cry. It was the most amazing thing. No time in between the scolding me and the crying. She just switched...like this... *(Snaps fingers.)* She was brilliant! *(Harry walks to door of sun room and checks to see if his father is either listening in, or peeking through keyhole. Harry then straightens up and continues his story to Margaret in a confidential tone.)* Mr. Sharp picked me up and sat me on top of a huge stack of Girl Scout cookie crates, so I'd be eye-to-eye with him...I was actually a little taller, looking down on both of them..."Your mother and I are in love with each other, son. It's a secret, an enormous secret. You mustn't tell anyone or you'll cause the most terrible trouble. We only want one single person in the world to know: You. Okay?" I kept that a secret, too. I never let on...See? He was open with me, honest. The truth hurt, but, I could take it because like Ibsen says in the play, "The truth beats the hell out of deception." Mr. Sharp figured that out on his own, too, 'cause we'd never done *The Wild Duck* in town before...Big John Sharp was something special for Gloucester, I can tell you that...so was my mother, for that matter. Two totally honest people..

MARGARET. Totally honest?

HARRY. Totally honest.

MARGARET. And you admire that.

HARRY. I truly do.

MARGARET. John Sharp and I slept together all through the

year of *Our Town*. We started the night of the first read-through and we kept doin' it every night after every rehearsal and every performance, two-three times, some nights. It was intense. *(There is a long, long, long pause.)*

HARRY. I'm not gonna' let this spoil my night. *(Harry goes in through the kitchen to a rear hallway and collects his coat, scarf, mittens. His knee suddenly "goes out." He limps. He dresses himself for the winter cold and returns to face Margaret.* NOTE: *Harry uses mitten clips.)* It's probably well below zero, now, and I'm goin' out in it. Maybe I'll even walk on the beach...Remember it this way: first his knee went out, and then the man himself! *(Harry exits out of rear door to house, slamming same closed, limping all the way. There is a pause. Sophie appears at top of stairs. At the same time, Nathan appears in doorway to sun room.)*

SOPHIE. Who went out?

NATHAN. I heard the door slam.

MARGARET. Your father and his knee. Your son and his knee. The Boss and the Boss' knee. *They're all out!*

NATHAN. It's pitch-black and freezing...

MARGARET. Grown men have been known to survive a walk on a winter's night, Pa...even in Gloucester. *(Sophie sits next to Margaret on steps. They share a smile. Nathan takes a cookie from a tin on top of the refrigerator.)*

NATHAN. He must be upset.

MARGARET. What did John Sharp's father do for a living?

NATHAN. Hmmm?

MARGARET. Big John Sharp...what did he actually do for a living?

NATHAN. Foreman on the line down at North Shore Fish ...Blind as a bat without his glasses...tall fella... *(Thinks.)* Died. Bum tick'ah...Who cares? *(Thinks; shrugs.)* I'm goin' back in. Last episode... *(Turns, starts to exit, thinks better of it; stops, faces Margaret again.)* No matter how bad you think you've got it, no matter how bad she thinks she's got it, no matter how bad I think I've got it...*none* of us has got it ten percent as bad as Oscar Wilde, and that's a fact. *(Nathan exits. Sophie and Margaret look at one another for a moment.)*

61

SOPHIE. Why'd he go out?

MARGARET. Your father? *(Sophie nods. Margaret shrugs.)* Dunno... *(Margaret gathers pie materials — apples, etc — and starts to make a pie. Sophie helps.)*

SOPHIE. I'm really worried about him, Mama... *(Pauses; Margaret looks at Sophie.)* Poppy...He seems...scared about something...I dunno...

MARGARET. How so?

SOPHIE. *(Looks around, then, confidentially.)* He can't seem to learn his lines, Mama. He can't seem to, I dunno, *concentrate.*

MARGARET. I'll just bet.

SOPHIE. Hmm? *(Margaret looks at Sophie; pauses, smiles.)*

MARGARET. You like bein' in the play, don't you?

SOPHIE. *The Wild Duck? Sure!* Gawwwd! It's a great part...It's great...All the kids are really envious. *(Pauses.)* I think acting in plays makes you special... *(Pauses.)* Everybody says so... *(Pauses.)* Grandma did it, you did it. I know you didn't *love* it, but, you did it. And both Poppy and Mr. Sharp said you were really really good, too...

MARGARET. Mr. Sharp said that?

SOPHIE. Oh he did. Poppy, too. They both said you were *brilliant* in *Our Town.*

MARGARET. Not much to the part in *Our Town.* Just up and down the ladder a few times then you die. That's about it.

SOPHIE. Don't you like acting, Mama?

MARGARET. Everybody can't be an actress, Soph. *Somebody's* got to be out front, watching, paying attention, right?

SOPHIE. I know what you mean. Rosie tells me to never stop including the audience. She says that everything we do, we do for them...

MARGARET. You like Rosie?

SOPHIE. Rosie? Oh, yuh. She's great. Remember her Blanche? She's a great, great, great actress. And she never stutters when she's acting, either. Never. It's just amazing!

MARGARET. It is amazing.

SOPHIE. Oh, yuh, 'cause sometimes, when she's upset about

something, she stutters wicked...but when she's acting—even just rehearsing—you'd never ever know. It's like me with my contacts. I'm blind as a bat without them around the house, but on stage I hardly need them. *(Pauses.)* I was thinking maybe Hedvig could be called a lead. You think so?

MARGARET. I think so, yuh. Hedvig and the duck. The duck's got the title role.

SOPHIE. And Poppy and Rosie and John and old Mr. Sims. They're all leads, too, I'd say, but, me, too. I think I am. This is my sixth play, if we count bein' a walk-on in *The Threepenny Opera*...and my first lead. Not too bad for a fourteen year old, huh?

MARGARET. I'd say you were doing very well...You finish your homework?

SOPHIE. School's easy. That's what I like about doing plays. They're really hard. Wicked, some of them.

MARGARET. Do you like Mr. Sharp...John?

SOPHIE. Sure, I guess. *(Pauses.)* He's kinda' scary...Do *you* like him?

MARGARET. Oh, well, sometimes yes, sometimes no...

SOPHIE. He likes you a lot. *(She squeals in a schoolgirlish tone.)* Gawwdd, I shouldn't be telling you this... *(Margaret replies in same schoolgirlish voice.)*

MARGARET. Whaaaaattt??

SOPHIE. Gawwwdd! Once Mr. Sharp was tellin' this story about bein' in love and stuff with somebody who didn't know he was...in love with her during some other play, in olden times...when he was young and all... *(Leans in confidentially.)* It turns out it was *you*... *(Giggles.)* Yess! It was amazing. Everybody was all worried because they thought that my feelings would get hurt, but, I loved it! I really did, Mama!

MARGARET. You did?

SOPHIE. Sure, I did! It was olden times, for one thing. For another, you didn't even know about it, so, what coulda' be'n wrong, right?

MARGARET. Yuh, well, that's true enough...

SOPHIE. And Mr. Sharp kinda' forgot who he was tellin' the

story to...you know, Poppy bein' your husband, and me bein' your daughter and all... *(Giggles.)* He actually called you "Mahhghee," with this wicked townie accent and all... *(Giggles.)* Poppy went all white. He was really upset! But, then Rosie talked to him, I guess pointin' out that I was there...then everybody got all concerned over me and I pretended, a'course, that I was bothered by it all...but, I loved it. I just really did...I just really *loved it*... *(Sophie looks up at Margaret, lovingly.)* You're so beautiful now. You must've been off the charts back then!

MARGARET. *(Laughs.)* Yuh, well, I was okay...

SOPHIE. There's this great picture of you up, still, from *Our Town*...you and Poppy on the ladder, so in love. Gawwwdd! It just makes me almost *cry!*

MARGARET. I guess your father musta' brought it in ta' put up, yuh. Most of the others burned in the fire...

SOPHIE. Grandpa took it...

MARGARET. Oh, yes. He took them all...

SOPHIE. He's a great photographer, isn't he?

MARGARET. He...has a talent, yuh.

SOPHIE. Poppy's great, too. All the kids tell me that their older brothers and sisters *love* having Poppy take their graduation pictures. Everybody loves Poppy...

MARGARET. Your father's a lovable guy.

SOPHIE. Oh, not that they don't love you, too, Mama. Everybody does. But, Poppy's...I dunno...He just fits in with kids wicked easy.

MARGARET. You'll get no argument from me.

SOPHIE. And he's a great, great photographer. Like Grandpa. It makes me so happy to see their show pictures up on the walls at the playhouse, side by side...to know that, you know, this family has *greatness*.

MARGARET. In this life, it's not greatness I would worry about, Soph, it's goodness.

SOPHIE. I want to be great in *The Wild Duck*, Mama.

MARGARET. You'll be wonderful, Sophie. I know you will...

SOPHIE. I don't want to be wonderful, Mama. I want to be *great*...

MARGARET. Well, you will be...for Gloucester.

SOPHIE. Oh, Gawwdd, I'm gonna' try my best...

MARGARET. How about your homework? You're gonna' have rehearsal all the rest of this week...This is s'pose'ta be your heavy homework nights. You promised...

SOPHIE. I'm the best student in my class...

MARGARET. How about Ben Webster? And Zoë Swensen? How about Winnie Bell?

SOPHIE. That's just recent...

MARGARET. Greatness has to represent somebody's true character. It can't just come in the corners of your life. It's got to come into every area, into the center...Greatness has to be *who you are.*

SOPHIE. That's really beautiful. What play is *that* from?

MARGARET. I dunno...I don't remember. One of 'em...

SOPHIE. I think you're right. I'll do my World History...

MARGARET. You have a test?

SOPHIE. Well, it's just a quiz...

MARGARET. When?

SOPHIE. It's just a *quiz!*

MARGARET. Oh, Gawd, tomorrow?

SOPHIE. Mama, it's only a quiz! Don't worry. *Ne pas...*worry. *(Sophie starts up the stairs.)*

MARGARET. Sophie? Can I ask you something? Something kind of big?

SOPHIE. Sure.

MARGARET. Just-between-us kinda'thing...

SOPHIE. Sure. I mean, we're a mother and daughter, right? *(She returns to table, sits.)* Sophie, if for some reason we ever, uh, had to...move away from Gloucester...would you?

SOPHIE. You mean like to New York, or Hollywood kind of thing?

MARGARET. Well, yuh, maybe...

SOPHIE. Grandpa and I were just talking about that...

MARGARET. You were?

SOPHIE. If I have to move, you know...for work...I'll do the

65

Broadway play or the Hollywood movie, but, then I wanna' come straight back home to Gloucester...in between jobs. I want to...have a normal life, with you and Poppy and Grandpa and all...

MARGARET. Yuh, well...

SOPHIE. Is that what you meant? *(Nathan enters from the sun room.)*

NATHAN. Is he back?

MARGARET. Not yet.

NATHAN. It's nine. The show's finished.

SOPHIE. Was it sad?

NATHAN. I guess, yuh. It seemed like it was gonna be...

SOPHIE. You didn't see the end?

NATHAN. Most of it.

SOPHIE. You fall asleep?

NATHAN. I dozed. No reason to stay awake for sadness. *(To Margaret.)* You hear anything, before, in the yard?

MARGARET. No...

NATHAN. Where do you s'pose he is, this kind of hour?

MARGARET. It's only nine o'clock...

NATHAN. Still and all... *(To Sophie.)* You study your World History? *(To Margaret.)* She got her final tomorrow, ya know... *(Margaret is surprised; she glares at Sophie.)*

SOPHIE. I've been studying all night!

NATHAN. Your mother quiz you? *(To Margaret.)* You be'n quiz-zen' her?

MARGARET. A little... *(To Sophie; playacting for Nathan's benefit.)* Go back up now and study...I'll come back up and quiz you again in a while...

SOPHIE. *(Overacts.) Morrrre???* Oooookayyyy...*Geees! (She stomps off, up the stairs.)*

NATHAN. You've gotta nag. It's the only way they learn. My mother nagged, his mother nagged, you nag. It's the only way any-body learns anything, believe-you-me... *(Suddenly, Harry enters, from the back door. His scarf covers his face.)* Who's in here? *(Sees Nathan.)* Oh. I wanna' talk to my wife, just the two of us, if you'll

66

excuse us, please...

NATHAN. *(Shows his palms.)* No problem... *(Exits, into sun room.)*

HARRY. I stayed out in the yard, the whole time.

MARGARET. Musta' be'n cold.

HARRY. My hands are numb, my face is numb...

MARGARET. How's yo'r knee?

HARRY. Numb.

NATHAN. *(Reenters.)* Sorry.

HARRY. *What? What'd'ya' want?*

NATHAN. I made a mistake goin' back in there. Show's over. I meant to go upstairs to my room...Sorry. *(Nathan shows his palms again, goes upstairs. There is a pause as Harry and Margaret watch him go.)*

HARRY. *(Rubs his hands together, blows into them.)* I could have died out there, you know? We're talking sub-zero conditions!

MARGARET. You want a cup of tea?

HARRY. Alright, sure...

MARGARET. *(As she makes tea.)* Hungry?

HARRY. No.

MARGARET. There's Chicken Pritikin...

HARRY. I'm not hungry.

MARGARET. It's here if you change your mind.

HARRY. Hot or cold?

MARGARET. *(Looks up from stove.)* Hm?

HARRY. The goddamn chicken.

MARGARET. Cold.

HARRY. Okay, sure, if it'll make you feel better, so you'll let up on me a little...

MARGARET. *(Gets chicken for Harry, who paces in kitchen.)* Anything with it?

HARRY. I said I wasn't hungry...

MARGARET. *(Puts chicken on table in front of him.)* Take what you want.

HARRY. *(Picks up chicken leg, absently.)* Did you think to come out looking?

MARGARET. For you? Tonight?

HARRY. Did it even cross your mind? *(Sophie appears at top of staircase, calls down.)*

SOPHIE. Is that Poppy?

HARRY. *(To Margaret.)* I don't want her down here...

MARGARET. *(Calls upstairs.)* He's home. Do your home-work, please...

SOPHIE. Where were you, Poppy?

HARRY. *(To Margaret.)* I refuse to talk to her...

MARGARET. What?

HARRY. *(To Margaret; icily.)* You heard me...

MARGARET. *(Calls upstairs.)* Do your homework, Sophie. I'll be up in a minute...

SOPHIE. Poppy, are you down there?

MARGARET. Sophie, *damn it!*

HARRY. I won't talk to her! I'm warning you! *(Sophie runs down the stairs. Margaret scolds her.)*

MARGARET. I told you...

SOPHIE. Poppy, where were you?... *(Sophie tries to hug Harry, who pulls back from her.)* Poppy! *(Harry moves to threshold into sun room, with his back turned to Sophie. Nathan appears upstairs.)* Mama, what's this about?

MARGARET. Go upstairs...

SOPHIE. Mama, what's happening?

MARGARET. Go up to your room!

NATHAN. *(Calls down to Sophie.)* Come upstairs, Sophie...

SOPHIE. Poppy, please...

NATHAN. Sophie...

MARGARET. Sophie! *(Sophie looks at Harry and runs, tearfully, upstairs.)* Did you have to?

HARRY. *(Turns; faces Margaret.)* I want to know if you think that your child has the right to live under my roof.

MARGARET. *What are you asking me? (Both flash a look upstairs to be certain they are not being overheard. Neither Nathan nor Sophie is visible.)*

HARRY. I want a straight answer. Is Sophie mine or his? Well?

68

MARGARET. I don't know...

HARRY. You don't *know?*

MARGARET. I don't... *(Shrugs.)* I just don't.

HARRY. How could you not know?

MARGARET. I didn't want to know. It wouldn't have made any difference.

HARRY. This is no house for me anymore! *(He eats bite of chicken leg redresses himself for the winter cold. Nathan steps forward from the shadows above, calls down to Harry.)*

NATHAN. You'd better think this over, Harold.

HARRY. Stay out'ta this!

NATHAN. You'd better think this through...Things are getting very real here...

HARRY. *(Screams.)* Don't you *fucking tell me what's real and what's not real! The parts of me that are like you are the parts I hate!*

SOPHIE. *(Offstage.)* Poppy! Poppy! *(Sophie steps forward, beside Nathan. Harry looks at his daughter and then at his father. He walks to Margaret.)*

HARRY. Deception...Deception... *(He pulls on his coat, pulls collar up.)* Everything in town is closed...It's probably five below zero, plus the wind chill factor...probably legally twenty below. This is great. This is just great... *(He pauses at door and makes his Ultimate Proclamation.)* Tell that child of yours I'm quitting the play. Tell her she's in a show that won't go on. You tell her that, Margaret...and then you tell her *why. (Harry throws his scarf a final ring around his collared neck, and he exits, slamming the door boldly. Sophie moans from above.)*

SOPHIE. Poppy! What if he doesn't come back again? Mama, what if he really quits the play and never comes back home again, ever?

NATHAN. He'll come back. He's just gonna sleep in the shop tonight. Don't worry. Trust me...

SOPHIE. *(Pulls away from Margaret; screams at her.)* What did you say to him that made him quit? Answer me! Tell me the truth! *Answer me!* I want to know the truth! *(Margaret cannot speak. She turns away; weeps.)*

THE LIGHTS DIM TO BLUE.

END OF SCENE 1.

(MUSIC IN: "There's No Business Like Show Business."*)

Scene 2

Music.

Late afternoon, the next day.

Lights up in the Budd home, upstairs and downstairs. Black "no-seam" rolled down as backdrop in studio, upstairs. John Sharp is alone, downstairs, looking about. He exits dining room and goes into sun room.

There is a moment's pause, with an empty stage.

John reappears in dining room, looks about, silently, mysteriously; and then goes up staircase.

He is now in upstairs studio. He looks about, settling on cage with the duck. He opens cage and pats the duck.

JOHN. *(Imitating Rocky Balboa.)* Yo, Hendrik, it's me: the director! *(He then closes cage. Suddenly, Sophie bursts through silence, entering from her bedroom.)*
SOPHIE. Poppy! Poppy! *(She sees John Sharp and is disappointed.)* Oh.
JOHN. Hello!

*See Special Note on Copyright Page.

70

SOPHIE. I...I thought it was my father...

JOHN. He'll be here.

SOPHIE. *(Sadly.)* I wish I knew that for sure...

JOHN. I just saw him...

SOPHIE. You *did?*

JOHN. Yup.

SOPHIE. Did he change his mind about quitting the play?

JOHN. I'm sure he will if we handle it well. You'll have to trust me...

SOPHIE. Where did he stay last night? I went to the shop, first thing this morning, before school. It was all locked up...

JOHN. My house.

SOPHIE. He did?

JOHN. He rang our bell at 9:30, last night, asked if he could sleep on the sofa.

SOPHIE. *(Thrilled.)* Ohhh, I'm so gladdd! *(She embraces John.)* I was so worried! *(John pulls Sophie closer to him. There is a moment in which Sophie becomes uncomfortable and tries to pull away.)*

JOHN. Don't ever worry, Sophie. Don't ever. I'll always be close by for you. I'm home, now...

SOPHIE. Please, Mr. Sharp...my arm!

JOHN. *(Realizes.)* Sorry... *(Sophie frees herself. John reaches across with his free hand and touches Sophie's cheek.)* You mustn't ever be frightened, Sophie. There are so many different people who love you. You'll never be left...alone. Never...

SOPHIE. Oh, I know that, Mr. Sharp...*John*...I do. It's just that Poppy never stays away... *(Tearfully.)* Is it my fault?

JOHN. Is what your fault?

SOPHIE. You know... *(Weeps; regains her composure.)* Sometimes I want to die... *(Pause.)* Sometimes I think I know what it is, that gets Poppy so upset...

JOHN. What's that?

SOPHIE. Sometimes...I think maybe I'm not *his*...

JOHN. How can *that* be?

SOPHIE. Maybe I'm adopted. Sally-Ann O'Donnell is definitely adopted. I mean, she's Vietnamese! Maybe I am, too...

71

JOHN. Vietnamese?

SOPHIE. *(Smiles.)* Nooo... *(Looks away again, unhappily.)* I got scared. I really did. I thought Poppy really moved away.

JOHN. The play will open and your father will be playing the supporting role. I promise.

SOPHIE. I'm really *relieved. (John pulls Sophie close to him again, this time she doesn't pull back.)*

JOHN. I want you to know that I love you very, very much, Sophie. If you ever need me...to be close with you...ever...you only need to come to me. That's for now and for life.

SOPHIE. I like you very much, Mr. Sharp...John. I'm really grateful that you cast me in the play...that you gave me my first real lead.

JOHN. You're an extremely talented young lady...nice too.

SOPHIE. *(Suddenly.)* How come you didn't cast one of the twins, Mr. Sharp? I mean, I was *amazed*, really, when I got the part. How come you didn't cast one of your own daughters?

JOHN. Oh, well... *(Smiles.)* ...A director can't just cast family because they're *family*. You have to go with the talent. You're much more talented than Patricia or Priscilla, so, I went with you...

SOPHIE. Oh, God, Mr. Sharp...John... *(Giggles.)* Don't ever tell them that!

JOHN. I did already.

SOPHIE. Noooo...

JOHN. I certainly did. Right after the auditions...You must never lie, in any form. *Especially* to family. Remember what we're learning from the play: "The Saving Lie is the enemy of Honesty..."

SOPHIE. Oh, I'll never lie about anything again, I promise! And whenever I lied before, I always told God about it, in my prayers.

JOHN. Do you still pray?

SOPHIE. Oh, sure. Every night. I was up half the night, last night, just praying and praying...for Poppy...

JOHN. I hope you'll pray for *me* some day, Sophie.

SOPHIE. Oh, I will, I promise!

72

JOHN. Sometimes, when we want to get people to show us their love, we have to hide our own love away. We have to make people come look for it, or they'll never really see it...never really trust it...When they finally find our love, they're so pleased, they show us their love.

SOPHIE. Is that why you went away to New Hampshire? So that Mrs. Sharp and Trisha and Cilla would have to...come find you and show you their love?

JOHN. You're very smart, Sophie...beautiful and smart...

SOPHIE. I want Poppy to know how much I love him. If he knew...how much I do...he'd never leave us... (Suddenly.) I don't want Poppy to go off for five years like you did. I'm fifteen. I'll be twenty by the time he comes back...I don't want him to go.

JOHN. I think there's a way so he doesn't ever have to leave...

SOPHIE. Tell me!

JOHN. Maybe, for starters, if you didn't show him so much love. Maybe if you held back a little...

SOPHIE. And showed more to Grandpa...or Mama? That kind of thing?

JOHN. Or to other people? Me...

SOPHIE. That might make him jealous...of you, I mean.

JOHN. And then what? (There is a pause. Sophie considers all this and, suddenly, smiles.)

SOPHIE. Oh, Mr. Sharp, you're such a great person! (Sophie hugs John again. Margaret has entered, downstairs. She calls up.)

MARGARET. Who's in the house?

JOHN. We needn't discuss any of this with your mother. She doesn't always think like us...

SOPHIE. (Nods agreement; calls down to Margaret.) I'm up here with Mr. Sharp. We're just going over lines... (Margaret goes quickly upstairs.)

MARGARET. I'm coming up. (Arrives upstairs.) I was alone in the shop. I had to stay till Grandpa relieved me. He'll close up... (Kisses and hugs Sophie.) How was your test?

SOPHIE. It was fine. It was easy. (Suddenly.) How come Trisha didn't tell me that Poppy slept at your house?

JOHN. *(Smiles.)* Maybe she didn't know. He got there late and slept late. We didn't have breakfast till long after the girls left for the bus...

SOPHIE. Yuh, but, wouldn't she have seen him sleeping in the living room?

JOHN. *(Smiles.)* That's not the only sofa.

MARGARET. He came by the shop.

SOPHIE. Is he...still mad?

MARGARET. He's still a little...upset.

SOPHIE. What's happening, Mama?

MARGARET. *(Flashes John a worried look.)* It's...complicated...

JOHN. I'm sure he was feeling pressured...with the play opening so soon...

SOPHIE. That must have been it. *(Smiles.)* When did he say he'd get here...home?

JOHN. They're late. He was picking Rosie up...

SOPHIE. What did Poppy *say*, Mama? Is he still really mad at me?

MARGARET. He'll...he'll get over it.

SOPHIE. What did I *do?* Is he talking to me again?

MARGARET. It's not you. He's upset with *me...*

SOPHIE. What did you do?

JOHN. Sometimes it's better not to ask too many questions, Sophie. Sometimes, it's better just to have some trust in people...in people you care about. *(Nathan enters downstairs.)*

SOPHIE. That's him! *(Calls down.)* Poppy?

JOHN. Now, Sophie, remember...

SOPHIE. *Poppy?* 's'that you?

MARGARET. *(Looks at John.)* Remember what?

SOPHIE. *(Remembers; looks at John, then Margaret.)* Mr. Sharp and I had a talk...

NATHAN. *(Calls up.) I'm hommme!*

SOPHIE. *(Unhappily.)* Oh: you...

NATHAN. Should I go out and come in again?

74

MARGARET. She thought it was Harry.

SOPHIE. I thought it was Poppy... *(Flashes a look at John; shrugs.)*

NATHAN. Don't I get a kiss?

SOPHIE. Sure... *(She runs down steps to Nathan. John and Margaret exchange a severe glance.)*

MARGARET. What did you tell her?

JOHN. Nothing you should worry about. Trust me. *(Sophie arrives downstairs, runs into Nathan's arms. Upstairs John is trying — and failing — to kiss Margaret.)*

NATHAN. *(Looks up to upstairs.)* Who's up there?

SOPHIE. Mama and Mr. Sharp...

NATHAN. Alone?

MARGARET. *(Calls down; guiltily.)* I'm coming down...

NATHAN. No word from your father?

SOPHIE. *(Sadly.)* No. Mr. Sharp says they're comin', though... *(Margaret exits upstairs, quickly; John follows, after putting duck back into its tiny cage. Margaret arrives first; faces Nathan.)*

MARGARET. Hi. Any customers?

NATHAN. *(Coldly.)* Is this why you were hurrying home?

MARGARET. I won't dignify that remark.

JOHN. *(Faces Nathan; smiles.)* How are you, Mr. Budd?

NATHAN. Peachy. *(To Margaret.)* No word from Harry?

MARGARET. Not yet. *(Sophie goes to rear window; looks out.)*

SOPHIE. It's pitch-black.

NATHAN. Of course, it's pitch-black. It's win'tah...*Four o'clock* it was pitch-black. We should have moved to California...thirty years ago!

SOPHIE. Doesn't it get dark in California?

NATHAN. It's three hours earlier in California. People are just finishing lunch in California...

SOPHIE. *(Straining at the window.)* What's taking them? I can't see anything, not even the moon. *(Knock on door; Rosie enters. She wears sunglasses.)* Rosie!

ROSIE. I drove ahead on my own.

SOPHIE. Why are you wearing sunglasses?

MARGARET. *(Looks at Rosie's sunglasses; she knows.)* You told Earl.

ROSIE. He knows I was out last night. *(She removes her sunglasses; her eye is blackened.)*

NATHAN. Does he know with who? *(To Margaret.)* I wanna' know if we have to call the police, that's all...

ROSIE. He doesn't know.

SOPHIE. What happened to your eye, Rosie?

JOHN. *(Looking at Rosie's eye, in disgust.)* This is testament of how far we've come from telling the truth as a matter of course...

SOPHIE. What happened to your eye?

JOHN. She fell down...

ROSIE. I tripped over a thing.

HARRY. *(Enters front door and hallway; yells.)* I'm in the house! *(Enters kitchen; Sophie runs to him, tries to embrace him.)*

SOPHIE. Poppppyyy!! *(Harry turns away.)*

HARRY. Please!

MARGARET. Harry!

JOHN. Sophie!

NATHAN. Harold!

HARRY. Tell her I'm fine. Tell her not to waste her time worrying... *(He goes to Rosie.)* I decided not to confront him yet.

ROSIE. Did you t..t..t..talk to him at all?

HARRY. It didn't *feel* right...the timing...he had a snow shovel and a pick. *(Rosie nods. Sophie moves to Harry again.)*

SOPHIE. Mr. Sharp said you slept on his sofa last night.

HARRY. Did he? *(Flashes a look at John.)* Sometimes you're hard ta figure... *(To Sophie.)* If that's what he said, then that's what I musta'done, right?

SOPHIE. Didn't you?

JOHN. Of course he did! *(To Harry.)* Don't you think she's a little young for this kind of thing, Harry?

HARRY. What's this you're givin' me?

SOPHIE. He said you'd come back to the play, too. He promised you weren't going to quit...

HARRY. *(To John.)* Try tellin' her the truth, okay?

JOHN. Come onnn, Harrrrryyyy...

SOPHIE. *What?* Oh, my God, *what?*

JOHN. *(To Sophie.)* He hasn't quite decided yet, Sophie. Now, honestly, isn't that exactly what I said to you? Didn't I tell you just that?

SOPHIE. Poppy, *please!* In eighty-one years, the Wingaersheek Players have never had to cancel a show! Not even one!

HARRY. Maybe John Sharp can take over my part, too. He can play his supporting part and my lead role, too...

SOPHIE. Poppy, please don't keep turning away from me...

JOHN. Sophie...

SOPHIE. I don't like that plan! *(To Harry.)* Poppy, please talk to me...

HARRY. Margaret!

MARGARET. Sophie, stay away from him...

SOPHIE. Poppy!

HARRY. Margaret!

MARGARET. Sophie, don't bother him!

SOPHIE. *(Sobs.)* I'm not bothering him! I'm trying to hug him! He's my father!

HARRY. I certainly am not!

SOPHIE. *What?*

MARGARET. Harry!

ROSIE. Harry, no!

NATHAN. Harold Allen Budd! *(There is a long pause. Sophie reels backwards.)*

SOPHIE. What did you *say,* Poppy?

HARRY. You heard me.

SOPHIE. Oh, Poppy, please...

ROSIE. I don't think you mean that, Harry...Tell her...I think you're confused...

HARRY. I know perfectly well what I'm saying.

MARGARET. *(Angrily; to Harry.)* You promised me you wouldn't do this!

SOPHIE. Poppy, please, give me a hug... *(Sophie pulls at Harry.)* Please, Poppy...

HARRY. Go away! Get off! No touches! *(Tries to push Sophie away; yells at Margaret.)* I told you to keep her away from me!

SOPHIE. *(Sobs.)* Poppy!

HARRY. Margaret!

NATHAN. Harold, I forbid this!

MARGARET. I will leave you, Harry. I swear I will!

HARRY. Fine, perfect, just what you should do. And take your child with you. She has no business staying in this house. She should be with her parents, not here! Not with me!

SOPHIE. *(Shrieks.)* Popppyyyyy!

MARGARET. *(Goes to Harry; grabs him.)* That is the god-damn limit!

ROSIE. *(To Sophie.)* Come here, darling. Come to me...

MARGARET. *(To Rosie.)* Don't you DARE touch my child!

HARRY. Margaret, for God's sake, control yourself!

MARGARET. *(To Rosie.)* You've got no right...

ROSIE. I've got every right. She's an actress!

MARGARET. Stay away from her!

ROSIE. She should have love and support! Not...*this!*

SOPHIE. What are you talking about, Rosie? *(Margaret throws Rosie's coat and purse at her.)*

MARGARET. That you would even show your face in my house after sneaking in here, getting into bed with my husband...with her father...and you call her "darling"? I'm sorry Earl hit you, Rosie, but stay away from my family! *(To John.)* And you, you grim shit, you have ideas about love and marriage! What are you all? Demented?????

SOPHIE. Oh...Goddd...Mama! *Don't! (Sophie covers her ears and eyes and runs upstairs.)*

HARRY. You've really upset her, Margaret. You've really upset your daughter...

MARGARET. *What? (Sophie grabs duck; goes into darkroom.)*

HARRY. There was really no need to start in...

JOHN. I think one of us should go up to Sophie...

HARRY. Which of us? You?

JOHN. Should we flip a coin?

78

HARRY. I'll fucking flip you! You phoney! You fake!! I'm gonna tell you something. Tuborg Beer isn't even Norwegian. It's Danish. It's printed all over the label! Hold me back, 'cause I'm going for him... *(Harry hides behind Nathan just in case.)*

NATHAN. Don't talk stupid, Harold. *(To all.)* I'll go up to my granddaughter. *I'll* handle this. Calm her down. Trust me. *(Nathan starts up the stairs. Nathan stops; turns and faces them all.)* You should all be ashamed. Every one of you... *(He goes upstairs; calling Sophie.)* Sophie... *(He disappears into the back of the upstairs room, still calling her.)* Sophie? Where are you? *(There is a moment's pause. Nathan tries Sophie's room; then his own; then goes to darkroom.)*

HARRY. What I will do is move out of Gloucester, complete-ly...once and for all. There's work for a talented photographer in Boston...New York...California. Plenty of theatres, too...

JOHN. You should stay home with your daughter, who needs you and who loves you...

HARRY. With my what?

JOHN. With your daughter...

HARRY. Do you swear that?

JOHN. Where has she lived for fifteen years? *(We see Nathan upstairs at darkroom door.)*

HARRY. What's where she's lived got to do with anything? Am I her natural father?

JOHN. What's that s'posed to mean, Harry? There are babies born by artificial insemination. Who's the *natural* father?

HARRY. Are you telling me I'm *not* her natural father?

JOHN. I'm telling you that you're her father and she's your daughter and that is *everything*...

MARGARET. Listen to him...Harry, listen to John...

NATHAN. *(Upstairs.)* Unlock this door, young lady! *(A gunshot sounds behind darkroom door. There's a stunned silence.)* Oh, my God...

MARGARET. Sophie!

ROSIE. Oh, my God, Harry!

MARGARET. If anything's happened to our daughter, Harry, I will never forgive you...

JOHN. *(Softly.)* Hedvig...

HARRY. Sophie... *(Cries out.)* SOOOOPPPHHHIEEEE! *(He runs up the stairs. They all follow. Margaret slumps against wall, upstairs. Rosie goes to her. Harry kicks door to darkroom open. He and Nathan run inside.)*

ROSIE. Ohh, Gawd, Margie, please, forgive me, I'll never go near him again. I promise you, Marg...please, oh, please, Margie... *(Sobs.)* I'm so sorry! *(Margaret looks at Rosie; they embrace.)*

HARRY. *(Offstage in darkroom.)* Sophie, oh, my God, Sophie, oh, God, oh, God...Wake up!

NATHAN. *(Offstage.)* Wake up, Sophie! Sophie!

HARRY. *(Offstage.)* Sophie, wake up, *please wake up!*

SOPHIE. *(Offstage, softly.)* Grandpa...Poppy...

HARRY. *(Offstage.)* She's okay! *(Harry and Nathan appear. Harry carries Sophie in his arms. Nathan carries the starter pistol: the prop from the play.)* Sophie's okay...

NATHAN. She just fainted...

HARRY. She shot a blank off at the duck...

NATHAN. A huge flame must've shot out'ta the pistol...

HARRY. The duck's dead.

NATHAN. The duck got burned to a crisp! Smells like a Chinese restaurant in there.

JOHN. I'll deal with this. *(Pauses at door to darkroom.)* I've buried a lot of animals in my day. *(Exits into darkroom. Sophie stirs, slightly. All touch her, lovingly, tussle her hair, etc.)*

HARRY. Sophie just fainted, but the duck is definitely dead...

NATHAN. Definitely.

HARRY. Sophie killed it.

NATHAN. Sophie killed the wild duck. *(MUSIC IN: "Comedy Tonight."*)*

LIGHTS DIM TO BLUE
END OF SCENE 2.

---

*See Special Note on Copyright Page.

80

Scene 3

Later, that night.

White "no-seam" is rolled down as backdrop in studio, upstairs. Harry and Nathan, at table. Harry snacks, heavily.

HARRY. I'm starving.

NATHAN. You must be...feeling pressured. Whenever your mother felt pressured, she ate. She had quite a hunger.

HARRY. She wasn't fat.

NATHAN. You're not fat.

HARRY. I'm not thin.

NATHAN. Your mother wasn't thin.

HARRY. *(Looks at watch.)* It's over now... *(Nathan looks up; Harry explains himself.)* The rehearsal. First night on the set, at the playhouse.

NATHAN. How could they rehearse without you or Sophie?

HARRY. Stage manager probably read our lines in...

NATHAN. She'll be good as new tomorrow...

HARRY. I hope.

NATHAN. Damn shame about the duck.

HARRY. Hell of a thing. I've always thought they should do gunshots on tape instead of live.

NATHAN. Huh?

HARRY. You always read about actors getting burned from blanks...the flame that shoots out.

NATHAN. Killed the duck. That's for goddamn sure.

HARRY. Nice little duck, too...

NATHAN. Where'd he bury it?

HARRY. John? I doubt if he could get a hole dug...pitch-black out...four feet of snow...icy, underneath, too...

NATHAN. Probably threw it in the ocean...

HARRY. Sure. They coulda' just chucked it right off the cut bridge, what with the strong current goin' through...

NATHAN. Be in Ipswich by now...

HARRY. Rockport, probably. I think the tide would carry it more North than South...

NATHAN. Depends...

HARRY. Nice little duck, too...

NATHAN. Took quite a singeing...

HARRY. Quite a what?

NATHAN. Looked pretty singed ta' me.

HARRY. That's not what I call a *singe*... *(Holds up cooked meat from plate.)* These meatballs took a *singeing*. The duck got blasted. Would'a been more merciful if the gun hadda actually be'n loaded...

NATHAN. Hell of a stench up there. Reminds me of when a bed catches fire from somebody smokin'...

HARRY. Pillows, probably...

NATHAN. Oh, yuh, *'course*... *(Margaret appears at top of staircase. Nathan looks up.)* She sleepin'?

MARGARET. Uh uh. She's takin' a bath. I told her she could come down for a while...

NATHAN. She won't get to sleep too easy...

HARRY. Don't tell her that, or she won't for sure. You used'ta do that to me all the time...

NATHAN. When?

HARRY. When I was little. Some noise or somethin' would sound outside and scare you, you used'ta say to me "That's gonna' keep you awake, frightened, tonight!"...

NATHAN. Go onnn!

HARRY. And I'd think "Oh, Gawwdd, I'm not gonna' sleep..."

NATHAN. I never did...

HARRY. And 'course, I'd stay awake... *(Margaret enters, goes to*

82

stove, turns on fire under tea kettle.)

NATHAN. I never did...

HARRY. "Did"? You still *do!* Night before last, there was no moon. What did you say to me?

NATHAN. "There's no moon"?

HARRY. "There's no moon. Pretty scary. That'll keep you awake for sure, Harold."

NATHAN. Go onnn!

HARRY. Didn't get to sleep till dawn! 'Course, you slept fine, I'm sure, knowin' I was up, keepin' a watch on things...

NATHAN. *(To Margaret, who has teacup in hand.)* This man's mad! *(Without speaking, Margaret returns upstairs. Both men stare after her, surprised.)* She's not saying much yet...to you, anyway.

HARRY. I saw that.

NATHAN. Your mother once went very nearly two months without talking to me...

HARRY. Margaret never would...

NATHAN. You can never tell, up front. Once you're in it, you know...

HARRY. I know Margaret...

NATHAN. You think I didn't know your mother?

HARRY. *(Shrugs.)* Yuh, well, maybe you didn't.

NATHAN. In this life, what you see and what you *report* you see, had damn well better be two very different things, or life isn't gonna' be much worth livin'...

HARRY. Yuh, well, maybe...

NATHAN. No "Yuh, well, maybe" about it, Harold. You wanna' have an accurate report of who we are...the Budd family? You wanna' take a hard, clear look at finite detail? 'Cause, if you do, I can give you a fairly high degree of accuracy, even for a man of my years. *(Pauses.)* You just stop me when you want. I'll start with you. *(Looks away a moment, then looks directly at Harry, again.)* Harold Allen Budd, half-Jew-half-Italian...born on Christmas Day, December 25th, 19...

HARRY. Wait a minute! Just wait a goddamn minute!

NATHAN. You stopping me?

83

HARRY. My birthday's November the 1st!

NATHAN. That's what we *told* you. The truth is, you were born on Christmas. Your mother decided on November 1st for your birthday. She figured that Christmas had'da be just about the *worst* day of the year for a kid to have a birthday: school's out, kids are with their families, no parties, no real presents...everybody woulda' be'n saying "Here, Harry, this is for Christmas *and* your birthday..." *(Smiles.)* She figured November 1st was perfect. School's just settling back in, kids are warmin' up ta' one another...a perfect time to throw a party in whose honor? *(Laughs.)* You had some wonderful birthday parties. I can tell you that... *(Smiles.)* Wonderful thoughtful mother, your mother... *(Suddenly.)* I'll tell you something else: you're not thirty-nine; you're thirty seven. We lied to you about your age. Your mother always felt that the people who were the most youthful-lookin' — the most babyish, really, well, *lived longest.* So, we decided to add two years on to your age, so you'd always look a little youngish... *(Smiles.)* She wanted to tell you the truth when you turned sixty. Sixty is a tough birthday and she figured it might make it special for you if we could spring the news: "Harry, you're not sixty: you're fifty-eight. For your birthday, we're giving you two extra years... *(Smiles.)* She was an unusual woman, you're mother. *(Simply,)* Want more? More finite detail?

HARRY. You're out'ta yo'r mind!

NATHAN. Let me tell you something, Harold. What killed your mother usually kills people in six months' time. Took nearly seven years before your mother felt too bad at all... *(Smiles.)* Took ten years in all before she packed it in...Before she told me to, you know, *end it* for her.

HARRY. Are you telling me that...?

NATHAN. Of *course!* Didn't it ever strike you that she died awful *sudden?* Big party...singing...dancing...a one-act play...and the next morning, she was gone. Didn't that ever strike you?

HARRY. *(Softly.)* No.

NATHAN. Of course not, Harold. That's not the way we brought you up. *(Simply.)* Now you go upstairs to those girls and you pretend that everything is fine. That's exactly what they're waiting for...

84

HARRY. You think so?

NATHAN. I know so.

HARRY. Papa, why did Sophie shoot the duck?

NATHAN. *(Smiles.)* She's an unusual woman, your daughter. She's like her grandmother.

HARRY. But, why did she shoot the duck?

NATHAN. It's all in the ending, Harry, like you said about a week ago. Real life was heading for tragedy. *Somebody* had to put a stop to it... There's a great tradition in our family, Harold: when real strength is wanted, it's a woman who flexes her muscles, *first...* then the men follow suit.

HARRY. But, why did she shoot the duck?

NATHAN. Jesus, Harold, pay attention! Sophie could see what was coming...so, she rewrote the ending. Who did Hedvig shoot? Who did Sophie shoot?

HARRY. Ohhhhhhhhhhh.

NATHAN. You got it.

HARRY. It wasn't a great idea to rehearse in the house, was it?

NATHAN. Good for you. *(Margaret and Sophie appear at the top of the stairs. Harry stands; wide grin.)*

HARRY. Hiiiiiiii.

SOPHIE. Hi.

HARRY. Couldn't sleep?

SOPHIE. Uh uh.

HARRY. Goin' over lines?

SOPHIE. What for?

HARRY. They had the stage manager reading in our lines for us tonight, but they expect us tomorrow... *(Sophie looks away; down.)* Oh, I changed my mind about quitting. A show's *gotta'* go on, right. And, oh, listen, Sophie, I have the most wonderful news: the duck's okay... *(Sophie looks at Harry.)* Singed and smelly, but on its way ta' bein' good as new...The duck is definitely a-okay!

SOPHIE. Poppy, are you *serious?*

HARRY. Oh, *yes!* I think he'll be back at rehearsal in two or three days. Well in time for the opening...but definitely good as new. No sign of anything wrong at all... *(Sophie runs downstairs into Harry's arms. Nathan and Margaret watch, smiling, as Harry embraces his daughter. Harry and Sophie are very nearly weeping.)* I'm so sorry, Sophie...I am. I hope you can forgive me.

SOPHIE. There's nothing to forgive. You're my father. *(Margaret stands on landing, looking down.)*

HARRY. Peg...I...I'll try to be better, Peg.

MARGARET. Don't try, Harry: *succeed!*

HARRY. I love our family so much, Peg...

MARGARET. Do you?

HARRY. Look at Sophie's eyes, Peg. They're just like mine, aren't they? *(Nathan looks at Harry; smiles.)* I mean it's really obvious, isn't it? Sophie's eyes are exactly — precisely — like mine. Most obvious thing in the world...like father, like daughter! Can you see it Soph?

SOPHIE. Oh, I do! I do! Everybody always says how much we look alike...two peas in a pod! *(Harry looks at Margaret; smiles. Margaret sniffs back a tear, bravely; looks at Harry, lovingly.)*

MARGARET. The Year of the Duck...

HARRY. I love you so much, Peg. I'm so sorry...

MARGARET. Me, too... *(Margaret and Harry kiss.)*

HARRY. *(To Nathan.)* All's well that ends well...

NATHAN. That's what they tell me... *(Sophie and Margaret embrace. Harry crosses to Nathan, speaks discreetly.)*

HARRY. You and I don't look very much alike at all, do we?

NATHAN. What do I know? I'm an old man. I think I'll be in there watching something. *(Yells.)* WHOOSH!! *(The television set starts up, magically, in the other room. We hear: voices singing "There's No Business Like Show Business,"* loudly. It is a stirring, conclusive piece of music. It swells and fills the auditorium. Nathan exits into the TV room. Harry, Sophie and Margaret embrace.)*

THE CURTAIN FALLS.

*See Special Note on Copyright Page.

86

THE PLAY IS OVER.

(NOTE: Sophie carries duck during curtain call, to "prove" to audience that the bird is still alive.)

I.H.,

New York City - Gloucester, Mass.,
June, 1985 - April, 1988.

PROPERTY LIST

ACT I
SCENE 1

ONSTAGE
Old-fashioned camera
Oversized round oak table
Oversized, old-fashioned Tiffany globe
Photos
Huge rolls of colored "no-seam" background papers
Dining room table
Garbage bin (foot pedal variety)
Beer

OFFSTAGE
Plates of food (Margaret)
Casserole
Cigarettes (John)
Dog-earred paper (Harry)

SCENE 2

ONSTAGE
Gun
Script
Cage

OFFSTAGE
Bag of groceries (Margaret)

ACT II
SCENE 1

ONSTAGE
Finished posters

2 chairs
Tin of cookies
Apple pie materials
Chicken Pritikin

SCENE 2

OFFSTAGE
Starter pistol (Nathan)

SCENE 3

ONSTAGE
Cooked meat on plate
Tea kettle
Teacup

COSTUME PLOT
(Costume Design by Mimi Maxmen)

SOPHIE BUDD
Ii — Striped T-shirt OVER
Wingaersheek Players sweatshirt
Turquoise cords
Tennis shoes
Socks
ADD yellow sweater for rehearsal

Hedvig dress
Wire rim spectacles
Pinafore
Cameo
Lace fichu

Iii — Long-sleeve, print T-shirt
Lavendar coveralls
Socks

IIi — Yellow cardigan sweatshirt
Sweatpants
Wingaersheek Players T-shirt
Socks

IIii — Lavendar coveralls
Pink cotton shirt

IIiii — Nightgown
Heavy socks

HARRY BUDD
Ii — Maroon ps/bd Oxford cloth shirt
Faded, cutoff sweatshirt

Brown dress slacks
Desert boots
Socks
T-shirt
Watch
Wedding band
Belt
PLUS beige smock

PLUS large fisherman's cardigan

Iii — Car coat
Hat
Mittens w/mitten clips
Scarf
Maroon cords
Tweed pullover sweater
Green T-neck

IIi, ii, iii — Maroon L.L. Bean
Green cords
Belt
Cardigan
Coat, etc.

MARGARET BUDD
Ii — Green wool tweed slacks
Pink turtleneck
Suede belt
Maroon tweed cardigan
Apron
Slippers
Socks
Watch
Rings

Iii — Peach knitted T-neck sweater
Jeans
Socks

IIi — Red plaid blouse
Moss green, patterned crewneck
Jeans

IIii, iii — Red pullover
White blouse
Plaid skirt
Tights
Boots
Earrings
Down jacket
Green mittens
Scarf
Hat

NATHAN BUDD
Ii — Brown cuffed suit slacks
Old brick plaid shirt
Loden green sweater cardigan vest
Off-color socks
Brogues
T-shirt
Wedding band
Belt

Iii — Same as Ii EXCEPT
Green/blue plaid shirt
Red/maroon cardigan

IIi — Slacks
Grey glen plaid shirt
Bathrobe

Slippers
Socks
Belt

IIii — Slacks
Hat w/earflaps
White w/brown striped shirt
Muffler
Old rubber boots
Suit jacket
Maroon sweater vest
Houndstooth check winter jacket

ROSIE NORRIS
Ii — Multicolored striped skirt
Fuchsia cotton T-neck
Magenta and black long pullover sweater
Boots
Character shoes
Tights
Earrings
Rings
Watch
Long scarf

Grey cape
Hat
Large scarf/shawl—uses over clothes at rehearsal (rose mohair)
Gloves
Multicolored scarf

Iii — Purple/black knit skirt
Turtleneck T
Long, blue sweater
Gold chains
Earrings

IIii — Black knit slacks
Green/black tweed turtleneck sweater
Lurex scarf/shawl

JOHN SHARP
Ii — Off-white, long-sleeve T
Plaid shirt
Orange zip-front, hooded sweatshirt
Black jeans
Work boots
White wool socks
Yellow/black plaid vest
Wedding band
Watch

Scarf

Hooded parka
Gloves

Iii — T-shirt
Long-sleeve, striped velour
Navy cords
Down vest w/scarf

IIii — Black jeans
T-shirt
Plaid shirt
Dark green work shirt
Down vest w/scarf

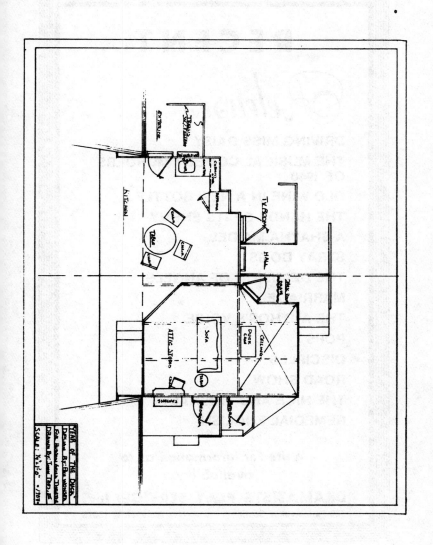

RECENT

Releases . . .

DRIVING MISS DAISY

THE MUSICAL COMEDY MURDERS OF 1940

OLD WINE IN A NEW BOTTLE

THE HANDS OF ITS ENEMY

A SHAYNA MAIDEL

STRAY DOGS

THE DELUSION OF ANGELS

MARRIAGE

THE AUTHOR'S VOICE

POPS

DISCIPLES

ROAD SHOW

THE NICE AND THE NASTY

REMEDIAL ENGLISH

Write for information as to availability

DRAMATISTS PLAY SERVICE, Inc.

440 Park Avenue South   New York, N.Y. 10016

0483   1090

NEW

Plays

STEEL MAGNOLIAS

THE LUCKY SPOT

THE DREAMER EXAMINES HIS PILLOW

BODIES, REST, AND MOTION

HOW TO SAY GOODBYE

JACOB'S LADDER

PASTA

MR. 80%

TRACERS

DANGER: MEMORY!

VANISHING ACT

PROGRESS

THE DREAM COAST

JITTERS

DRAMATISTS PLAY SERVICE, INC.

440 PARK AVENUE SOUTH   NEW YORK, N.Y. 10016